Portrait of Thomas Middleton from Dyce Collection 25 E 46 reproduced by courtesy of the Board of Trustees of the V & A

The Witch

THOMAS MIDDLETON

Edited by
ELIZABETH SCHAFER
Royal Holloway, University of London

LONDON/A & C BLACK

NEW YORK/W W NORTON

First published 1994
A & C Black (Publishers) Limited
35 Bedford Row, London WC1R 4JH
ISBN 0–7136–3945–8

Published in the United States of America by
W. W. Norton & Company, Inc.
500 Fifth Avenue, New York, NY 10110
ISBN 0–393–90073–8

A CIP catalogue for this book
is available from the British Library
and the Library of Congress.

Typeset in 10pt Plantin by Selwood Systems, Midsomer Norton

Printed in Great Britain
by Biddles of Guildford Limited

CONTENTS

ACKNOWLEDGEMENTS

Thanks to Richard Allen Cave, Richard Proudfoot, Ian Spink, David Ward and the general editor, Brian Gibbons, for comments and suggestions, and to William C. Carroll for his article on the author.

ABBREVIATIONS

Editions of the play cited

Revels	*Three Jacobean Witchcraft Plays*, ed. Peter Corbin and Douglas Sedge, Revels Plays Companion Library (1986)
Dyce	*The Works of Thomas Middleton*, ed. A. Dyce (1840)

Periodicals and reference works

Chambers	E. K. Chambers, *The Elizabethan Stage* (1923)
Grove	*The New Grove Dictionary of Music and Musicians*, ed. Stanley Sadie (1980)
Masque of Queens	Ben Jonson, *Masque of Queens*, ed. C. H. Herford, Percy and Evelyn Simpson, vol. 7 (1941)
NQ	*Notes and Queries*
OED	*Oxford English Dictionary*
Scot	Reginald Scot, *The Discovery of Witchcraft*, reprint of the 1584 edition (1973)
Tilley	M. P. Tilley, *A Dictionary of Proverbs in England in the Sixteenth and Seventeenth Centuries* (1950)

Works by Middleton

CM	*A Chaste Maid in Cheapside*. All references to the works of Middleton are to A. H. Bullen's 8-volume edition (1885).
s.d.	stage direction
s.h.	speech heading

Shakespeare references are to *The Riverside Shakespeare*, ed. G. Blakemore Evans (1974).

INTRODUCTION

THE AUTHOR

THOMAS MIDDLETON lived and worked in London nearly all his life.[1] Born in 1580, he was christened at St Lawrence Jewry on 18 April, and was buried on 4 July 1627 at his parish church in Newington Butts, where he had lived from at least 1609. His father, William, was a bricklayer and gentleman with his own coat of arms; he died in January 1585/86, and in November 1586 his widow, Anne, married Thomas Harvey, who had just returned, impoverished, from a voyage to Virginia. Within weeks of the marriage, Harvey was revealed to be an unscrupulous adventurer, almost solely interested in gaining control of his wife's estate. A protracted, confusing and ugly series of lawsuits engulfed the family over the next two decades, all beginning with Harvey's attempt to take over the property which Anne had put in trust for her children before she met him. Allen Waterer, who married Middleton's sister, Avis, in 1596, immediately became a party to the lawsuits as well. By 1603, when both Anne Harvey and Allen Waterer died, Middleton had spent a good part of his time assisting his mother in the various legal battles. Even after Waterer's death, Avis and her second husband, John Empson, continued legal action over the family property.

Middleton's life was early and frequently connected to the professional theatre. A large part of the family property at question in the various lawsuits was 'the grounde called the Curteyn where now comenlye the Playes be playde' – that is, the Curtain Theatre (built in 1577). After matriculating at Queen's College, Oxford (the most popular college of the time) in April 1598, moreover, Middleton was forced in June 1600 to convey his half-share of the Curtain property to his brother-in-law Waterer for money 'paid and disbursed for my advauncement & preferment in the university of Oxford where I am nowe a student'. Some time during the next eight months, however, he had to return to

[1] The chief facts of Middleton's life have been set forth in two articles by Mark Eccles: 'Middleton's Birth and Education', *RES* 7 (1931), 431–41, and '"Thomas Middleton A Poett"', *SP* 54 (1957), 516–36. Virtually all the facts in this commentary derive from Eccles. I have also found useful R. C. Bald, 'Middleton's Civic Employments', *MP* 31 (1933), 65–78; Mildred G. Christian, 'A Sidelight on the Family History of Thomas Middleton', *SP* 44 (1947), 490–6; and P. G. Phialas, 'Middleton's Early Contact with the Law', *SP* 52 (1955), 186–94.

London to deal with the continuing series of lawsuits, and it was reported, as of 8 February 1600/1, that Middleton 'remaynethe heare in London daylie accompaninge the players'. In a final twist, Middleton's brother-in-law Thomas Marbeck was an actor for the Admiral's Men; Middleton thus may have met his wife through this association. Middleton in any event never graduated from Oxford, and was already a professional playwright at the time he would have been receiving his diploma.

Since his son Edward was aged nineteen in 1623, we assume Middleton was married about 1602. His wife, Magdalen (she is 'Maria' or Mary in one document), was the granddaughter of the famous composer and organist John Marbeck; Eccles believes she was probably the Maulyn Marbeck christened on 9 July 1575 at St Dunstan's in the West. Middleton's widow petitioned in February 1627/28 for a gift of money from the city of London, which suggests that his estate had been small. She died five months later, in July 1628, and was also buried at Newington.

Middleton published one book of verse, *The Wisdom of Solomon Paraphrased* (1597), before he entered Oxford, and two more, *Micro-Cynicon* (1599) and the *Ghost of Lucrece* (1600), while presumably still a student. In 1602 Henslowe recorded that he was working on three plays: a collaboration with Dekker, Munday, Drayton and Webster on *Caesar's Fall* (now lost); *Randal, Earl of Chester* (also lost); and an unnamed play. Two years later, in 1604, he published two satiric prose pieces, *The Black Book* and *The Ant and the Nightingale*. His earliest surviving play, *The Family of Love* (*c.* 1602–3), also dates from this period. If the quality of these early works is debatable, it is clear that, after he left Oxford, Middleton was both an active and a highly productive writer. Beginning in 1613 and continuing until his death, he also wrote a number of civic pageants and entertainments; as early as 1604, he had written a speech given as part of Dekker's *The Magnificent Entertainment* for King James's official entry into London. Middleton was appointed City Chronologer in 1620, to record the memorable acts and occurrences of the city; he was succeeded in this position by Ben Jonson.

Middleton wrote in a variety of genres, but his greatest achievements came in two distinct dramatic forms: (1) city comedies, including *Michaelmas Term* (*c.* 1605), *A Mad World, My Masters* (*c.* 1605), *A Trick to Catch the Old One* (*c.* 1606) and *A Chaste Maid in Cheapside* (*c.* 1611–13); and (2) tragedies, including *The Revenger's Tragedy* (*c.* 1606–7), *Women Beware Women* (*c.* 1621) and *The Changeling*, with William Rowley (1622). Middleton's accomplishments in tragicomedy – *The Witch* (*c.* 1615), *A Fair Quarrel* (*c.* 1615–17) and *The Old Law* (1618), among others –

were also substantial. In 1624 he wrote the political satire *A Game at Chess*, which had the longest consecutive run of any play in the Jacobean period (indeed, the first long run in English theatrical history), nine days at the Globe, and caused a sensation in London; the play was finally suppressed by the government, though it had been properly licensed. Middleton and the players were summoned before the Privy Council (his son Edward answered for him, as Middleton seems to have been lying low), but no action was taken.

Middleton wrote for the children's companies of Paul's and Blackfriars, and after they disbanded, for Prince Henry's (formerly the Admiral's) Men, the Lady Elizabeth's company, and for Shakespeare's company, the King's Men. He collaborated on plays with many other dramatists of the period, possibly with Shakespeare himself on *Timon of Athens*, and seems to have revised Shakespeare's *Macbeth* some years after its first performance.[2] From his inheritance in The Curtain to his pageants for the city, Middleton's whole life traces the arc of the recently invented career of the professional playwright.

WILLIAM C. CARROLL

DATE

I believe *The Witch* to have been written in 1615–16. The manuscript states that the play was 'long since acted, by his majesty's servants at the Black friars'. This 'long since' has to be placed by the date of the manuscript, which is likely to be between 1619 – the date of the first recorded dramatic transcript by Ralph Crane, the scribe who produced the manuscript – and 1627, the date of Middleton's death. (Although the manuscript is not signed by Middleton, the epistle suggests that he was personally involved with it.) The play is likely to date from after 1609–10, as before that date 'his majesty's servants', that is the King's Men, Shakespeare's theatre company, did not use the Blackfriars theatre. Middleton seems to have started writing regularly for the King's Men around 1614–15.

Some have argued that *The Witch* was influenced or inspired by Ben Jonson's *Masque of Queens* (presented on 2 February 1609). More recently commentators have dated the play between 1613 and 1616, believing it to be related to a contemporary scandal involving the Howard family, the Earl of Essex, Robert Carr, a Scottish favourite of James I and later Earl of Somerset, and Sir Thomas Overbury. The evidence for this is summarised

[2] See pp. xiv–xv.

in the section below on topical satire (pp. xv–xix). I believe that *The Witch* was written late in the Overbury affair as deliberate, particularised and dangerous satire which was suppressed by the government before it could have the sort of success Middleton was to have later with another political satire, *A Game at Chess*.

In his Oxford edition of *Macbeth* Nicholas Brooke discusses the dating implications of the music written for the songs in *The Witch*.[3] One song, 'Come away, Hecate!', which also appears in *Macbeth*, appears with music in a collection in which most of the music is known to be by Robert Johnson, who worked for the King's Men from 1609 to around 1615. The other song in *The Witch* that has its original music, 'In a maiden-time professed', is by John Wilson, who was born in 1595 and worked for the King's Men from around 1615 onwards. The fact that he composed the music for this song suggests a date for *The Witch* around 1613–15 because he would have been too young to be working for the King's Men much earlier (the earliest music known to be by him dates from 1614). The intersection between these two careers suggests a date for *The Witch* that also fits in logically with the tragicomedies Middleton was writing around 1615–16, such as *A Fair Quarrel*.

Middleton's play *A Chaste Maid in Cheapside* (*c.* 1613) also offers several analogues with *The Witch*: the comic construing joke of II.ii. (cf. *CM* I.i.65–77); the emphasis on drink in Francisca's lying-in (cf. *CM*'s treatment of Mistress Allwit's delivery); the casual abandonment of Francisca's unwanted baby (cf. *CM* II.ii); and the duke unexpectedly rising from the dead (cf. the rising up from the dead of Moll and Touchwood junior).

If *The Witch* was written and suppressed around 1615, the revival of interest in the scandal about Frances and Carr when they were released from the Tower in 1622 may have inspired the dedicatee Thomas Holmes's interest in the play. Equally the success of the satire of *A Game at Chess* (1624) may have stirred his interest in an earlier politically sensitive play written by the same author. Andrew Gurr points out that plays which survive in manuscript form are often controversial ones;[4] the fact that *The Witch* was written on the same batch of paper as one of the manuscripts of *A Game at Chess* suggests an association with this extremely controversial play.[5]

[3] *Macbeth*, ed. Nicholas Brooke (1990), p. 65

[4] Andrew Gurr, *The Shakespearean Stage, 1574–1642*, 2nd ed. (1987), p. 170

[5] W. W. Greg and F. P. Wilson, *The Witch*, Malone Society Reprint (1949), p. viii

SOURCES

The main source for much of the witchcraft material in *The Witch* is Reginald Scot's *Discovery of Witchcraft* (1584), a humane and intelligent book that treats witchcraft sceptically: it argues that many of the women executed as witches were in fact senile, confused or brow-beaten. Scot's book was burnt in the Scotland of James VI as an outlawed and heretical treatise, and the king wrote *Demonology* (1597, reprinted in 1603 as soon as James became King of England) in part to refute Scot.[6] Middleton often uses Scot verbatim, as will be seen from footnotes to the witch scenes, especially I.ii. Although no audience would recognise Scot as Middleton's source, the fact that when Middleton wanted detail on witch practices he went to a sceptical source is suggestive of his general strategy in this play, which I believe to be satiric.

The Witch also uses Thomas Bedingfield's 1595 version of Machiavelli's *Florentine History* as a source for the story of the duchess's revenge for being forced to drink from a cup made of the skull of her father. G. B. Cinthio's 4th novella of the fourth day in *Hecatommithi* (1574) has been identified along with Tourneur's *The Atheist's Tragedy* as a source for Isabella's story and the plot of the woman tricked into a never-to-be-consummated marriage when she is presented with faked evidence that her true love is dead.[7] Jonson's *Masque of Queens* has been suggested as a source of witch material and also possibly of costumes (hypothetically used in the masque and then passed on to the actors to be used in the first performance of *The Witch*); however, much of the common ground between the *Masque of Queens* and *The Witch* seems unremarkable given their shared interest in presenting witches on-stage. Virgil's *Eclogues* 8 is clearly a source for the love charm in II.ii, and the text Middleton used has been identified through the mistake he copied from it.[8] Contemporary scandal (the Overbury affair) also constitutes a source.

[6] James's 'Preface to the Reader' makes it clear he is disputing 'against the damnable opinions' of Scot.

[7] For *The Atheist's Tragedy* as source see Anne Lancashire, '*The Witch*: Stage Flop or Political Mistake?' in '*Accompaninge the Players*', *Essays in Celebration of Thomas Middleton, 1580–1980*, ed. Kenneth Friedenreich (1983), pp. 166–8, and David George, 'The Problem of Middleton's "The Witch" and its Sources', *NQ* 212 (1967), 209–11. Also see George for an account of Middleton's use of Cinthio.

[8] Pierre Le Loyer's work, translated as *A Treatise of Specters* by Z. Jones (1605) has 'nodo' for 'modo', a mistake Middleton reproduces in II.ii.14. This is discussed in Gareth Roberts, 'A Re-examination of the Sources of the Magical Material in Middleton's *The Witch*', *NQ* 221 (1976), 216–19.

Macbeth is in some ways a source for *The Witch*, but the relationship between the two plays is very complex. Until recently critics have constructed the relationship in ways which worked to the disadvantage of Middleton's play. Because *The Witch* was believed to have failed in the theatre, the fact that it shares two songs and some dialogue with *Macbeth* was interpreted as proving that *Macbeth* was damaged by the 'inferior' material that Middleton added to it when he revised it in 1609 or 1610. The traditional view was that Shakespeare could not have authorised such interpolations. It is true that the songs fit more closely with the characters and situations of *The Witch* than with those of *Macbeth*, but it is simplistic just to disparage Middleton's interpolations, as so many editors of *Macbeth* have done. Recently the opposite critical approach to these passages has appeared. For example, Anne Lancashire, after arguing that the artistic merit of *The Witch* has been undervalued, suggests (p. 174) that after the play was suppressed, *Macbeth* was revived partly to keep *The Witch*'s political satire in circulation. Inga-Stina Ewbank follows Lancashire's lead, noting how the first Jacobean audience could see *The Witch* 'in the same playhouse and with the same cast' as 'they had seen the tragedy of *Macbeth*'.[9]

The two songs that appear in both the Folio text of *Macbeth* and *The Witch* are 'Come away, Hecate!' (*Macbeth* III.v; *The Witch* III.iii) and 'Black spirits' (*Macbeth* IV.i, *The Witch* V.ii). In neither case does the Folio text of *Macbeth* provide the full text of the songs, and until the two recent Oxford editions most editors of Shakespeare followed suit.[10] Consequently these songs are rarely performed as part of *Macbeth*.

Brooke's edition of *Macbeth* is remarkable for taking the songs from *The Witch* seriously, and he proposes the following hypoth esis: Middleton wrote 'Come away, Hecate!' when he was revising *Macbeth* in 1609–10, and in 1615, when he was writing *The Witch*, he reused the song. (Brooke (p. 58) cites R. V. Holdsworth's work on other instances of Middleton's reuse of songs from plays he had written earlier.) This theory also fits what we know about the music composed for *The Witch* (see p. xii) by Robert Johnson ('Come away, Hecate!') and John Wilson ('In a maiden-time professed'). The use of two different composers suggests that they collaborated or worked at different periods. Brooke favours the latter theory, suggesting that when Middleton

[9] Inga-Stina Ewbank, 'The Middle of Middleton', in *The Arts of Performance in Elizabethan and Early Stuart Drama: Essays for G. K. Hunter*, ed. Murray Biggs et al. (1991), p. 157. The subject of Middleton's possible contributions to both *Timon of Athens* and *Measure for Measure*, aired first as part of the Victorian vogue for authorship controversy, has recently been revived.

[10] See Brooke and *The Oxford Complete Shakespeare*, ed. Stanley Wells et al. (1988).

came to write 'his entertainingly bawdy burlesque of witchcraft' in *The Witch*, he already had a 'cast and themes to develop' from his work on *Macbeth* (p. 66).

The relationship between *The Witch* and *Macbeth* is rendered still more complicated by the fact that two possible mistakes in Ralph Crane's transcription of *The Witch* – e.g. III.iii.71: 'steepe' for 'steeple'; V.ii.70: 'againe' for 'a grain' – can be deduced from William Davenant's Restoration adaptation of *Macbeth*, which includes the Hecate additions and songs. Davenant worked for the King's Men in the 1630s, and it is assumed that he used a playhouse copy of *Macbeth* as the basis for his adaptation.

TOPICAL SATIRE

A summary of the sensational events of the scandal involving Frances Howard, the Earl of Essex, Robert Carr and Sir Thomas Overbury will help demonstrate their relevance to *The Witch*.[11]

Frances Howard was married to Robert Devereux, Earl of Essex, in 1606, when she was thirteen and he was fourteen. Because of their youth, the marriage was not consummated, and the Earl went travelling in Europe. When he returned in 1609 Frances was no longer interested in him. She had been leading a lively existence at court and may have had an affair with Prince Henry, James I's eldest son, before starting an affair with Robert Carr. On 25 September 1613, Frances secured a divorce from Essex – after much active support and lobbying by James I – and on Sunday, 26 December 1613, Frances married Carr. The wedding celebrations included a masque by Middleton (now lost) called *The Masque of Cupid*.[12] The grounds for the divorce were that Essex was subject to witchcraft and could not have sex with his wife, although he was not rendered incapable in relation to other women. The claim that Essex had been bewitched occasioned much gossip, particularly because the 'proof' included a test for Frances's virginity; she was physically examined by several women, but the fact that she appeared for the examination veiled led to speculation that she knew she could not pass the test and persuaded another woman to take her place.

It was subsequently discovered that Frances had paid various

[11] See Beatrice White, *Cast of Ravens: The Strange Case of Sir Thomas Overbury* (1965). For ease of reference the woman who was at various times Frances Howard/Essex/Somerset will simply be designated 'Frances' in this introduction.

[12] The marriage was not popular. See A. A. Bromham and Zara Bruzzi, *'The Changeling' and the Years of Crisis, 1619–24* (1990), p. 22. They comment that the masque was produced 'for the banquet which James insisted the City should provide'.

people to practise witchcraft against Essex and also by witchcraft to bind Robert Carr's affections to her alone. These dealings came to light in the course of the investigation into the death of Sir Thomas Overbury (d. September 1613), a close associate and probably lover of Carr for many years, who had implacably opposed Carr's marriage to Frances. Frances had paid for witchcraft against Overbury, but when she found that this was not working, she attempted to have him poisoned. It is unclear what role Carr played in this; he always maintained his innocence, and it is possible that Overbury died from the effects of potions he was taking through choice at the time. Those who had attempted to poison Overbury, Frances's accomplices, were all executed, but when both Carr and Frances were tried in 1616 and found guilty, they were merely sent to the Tower. They were released in 1622, shortly before Middleton and Rowley's play *The Changeling* was licensed. *The Changeling* may indicate a renewed interest in the scandal as it seems to make reference to it – most obviously in the virginity test of IV.i.[13]

The intersections between this scandal and *The Witch* can be summarised as follows:

a) A woman of murderous inclinations named Frances/ Francisca. There is the pun Frances Carr/Francisca, if the last syllable of 'Francisca' is stressed.

b) A separation between a man (Antonio, Essex) and wife (Isabella, Frances) to allow the remarriage of the wife (to Sebastian, Carr) as a virgin in circumstances where the fact of the virginity is stressed and is supposedly a result of the first husband being bewitched.

c) Sensational poisoning narratives. The duchess tries to murder her husband; Frances was rumoured to have attempted to poison Essex. The duchess attempts to murder Almachildes because he is in the way of her marriage to the Lord Governor, which would be politically advantageous for her. This parallels the attempt by Frances to have Overbury, the underling who opposed her marriage to Carr, murdered.

d) A court environment like that of James I.

e) An interest in love charms. The charms Almachildes uses to win Amoretta are like those Frances used to secure Carr's attentions. In order to stress the love charm element, Middleton was willing to allow the plot to creak audibly (the coincidence of Amoretta and the duchess having the same names). This suggests that Middleton's main focus was not plausible narrative but topical satire.

[13] See Bromham and Bruzzi; J. L. Simmons, 'Diabolical Realism in Middleton and Rowley's *The Changeling*', *Renaissance Drama* 11 (1980), 135–70, especially pp. 153–5.

f) Apparent references to the scandal: II.ii.131–3 – 'best folks' get away with anything (see also V.i.93–4, IV.i.51–3); V.i.51 – 'strong bill of divorcement'. Almachildes recommends a test for virginity (III.i) before any man embarks on marriage. There is also a general obsession with female virginity and chastity in the play. Amoretta reflects on being a 'perfect' maid rather than a 'cunning' (i.e. false) one (II.ii.74–6). In IV.i.44 there is a reference to 'spoon-meat' as a vehicle for poison, as was believed to be the case in Overbury's death. There is a possible reference in III.ii.66 to the famous wise man Simon Forman, who was embroiled in Frances's schemes against Overbury.

Margot Heinemann suggests that *The Witch* was specifically written with the interests of an anti-Carr patron in mind – a man such as the Earl of Pembroke, who became Lord Chamberlain after Carr's fall and who has been suggested as the patron of the daring performance of the satire *A Game at Chess* later in Middleton's career.[14] Reading *The Witch* as being actively and overtly political is certainly plausible in terms of Middleton's writing career. He started his career as a playwright writing for The Children of Paul's, who were famous for their repertoire of satirical plays.[15] He represented a real person (Mary Frith) on the stage in his play (with Dekker) *The Roaring Girl*, and Anne Lancashire has argued that he is the author of the 'politically charged' *Second Maiden's Tragedy*.[16] He also wrote about the contemporary malaise of duelling in *A Fair Quarrel*. *A Game at Chess* is a very interventionist and particularised attack on clearly recognisable members of James's court and is also based on a historical incident, a trip to Spain by Prince Charles and Buckingham. Middleton was clearly a politically committed playwright with Protestant sympathies who would relish satirising Frances's misfortunes, since she was both a murderer and a member of the extremely powerful pro-Catholic Howard faction. The emphasis on satire also explains why the play is not popular today: the topical satire which was once its strength is now largely lost. Similarly, *A Game at Chess*, once a nine day's wonder, the longest running theatre hit of the Renaissance, is no longer popular because the target of the satire is now obscure.

Even when it is accepted that *The Witch* satirises the Howard/Essex/Carr scandal, critics still argue over what stage in the proceedings had been reached when the play was written. Anne Lancashire proposes that it alludes to the divorce scandal,

[14] *Puritanism and Theatre: Thomas Middleton and Opposition Drama under the Early Stuarts* (1980), pp. 108, 111

[15] See Reavley Gair, *The Children of Paul's: The Story of a Theatre Company, 1553–1608* (1982). Gair points to contemporary allusions in *The Phoenix* by Middleton (p. 152).

[16] '*The Witch*: Stage Flop or Political Mistake?', p. 163

with its rumours of witchcraft and love potions, but suggests that as the Overbury murder story began to break, the play became too dangerous to stage; by 1615–16 in the real-life scandal 'murder and poison overshadowed impotence in marriage' (p. 166). Because the first reference to Frances as a poisoner occurred as early as 1610, Lancashire can argue for a very early date for the play. This she needs to do because she reads the end of the play as masque-like and reformative, and this ending would have appeared an outrageous 'whitewash' (p. 172) by the time the details of the Overbury murder were emerging. I feel that Bromham and Bruzzi are closer to the tone of the play when they describe *The Witch* not as 'reformative' but as 'exud[ing] a sense of disgust that is barely held in control by the dramatist' (p. 25). They are also convincing in drawing parallels between the progress of three of the female characters in *The Witch* and various aspects of Frances's career (p. 26). Elsewhere Bromham argues for a date before the full details of Overbury's murder emerged in 1615, but the play could be seen to be responding to events late in the scandal. In particular the forced happy ending of *The Witch* could be understood as reflecting on the happy ending engineered for the aristocratic criminal Frances, who retired to live in some splendour in the Tower while her accomplices were executed.[17]

I also believe that the court of James is being satirised generally, well beyond the particularities of Frances's schemes. For example, the king's interest in witchcraft was well known but, instead of pandering to royal tastes, Middleton presents witches as such comic bogies that he seems to be parodying the royal interest. Another favourite royal pastime satirised in several episodes of the play is drinking to excess. Too much alcohol is to blame for the duchess's story which begins with a drunk's insult to his wife; in I.i. Almachildes decides when under the influence of alcohol to visit the witches; many characters suffer from a 'surfeit' or excess, usually of drink and food; and in the manuscript there is also a revealing slip in the opening scene, where there is a reference to a drunken 'king', not a drunken duke, as it should be. This mistake follows a source, Bedingfield's version of Machiavelli's *Florentine History*, but it is also suggestive of the notoriously heavy drinking at James I's court.[18] The inclusion of

[17] A. A. Bromham, 'The Date of *The Witch* and the Essex Divorce Case', *NQ* 225 (1980), 149–52

[18] Condemnations of heavy drinking appear at: I.i.32, 35, 40–1, 43–5, 87, 89, 96, 106, 108; I.ii.84; II.ii.2. Surfeits of eating and drinking are commented upon at I.i.34, 137 and II.i.77, and Francisca's (fictional) prospective bridegroom is plausibly reported at III.ii.71 as having died of a surfeit. For heavy drinking at James's court

a character with a Scottish accent (II.i.171) in a play set in Ravenna also glances at James and his Scottish favourites, in particular Carr, who spoke broad Scots.

THE PLAY

Witch plays were popular in the early seventeenth century, a period of appalling witch-hunts in Europe.[19] Some of these plays claim to approach social history and adopt a pseudo-documentary approach; *The Witch of Edmonton* and *The Late Lancashire Witches*, for example, report on recent, notorious trials. Middleton's play is not, however, about the women who were executed for being 'real' witches in the witch-hunts. Instead, it shows larger than life, often rumbustious, quite comical singing witches who are never in any danger of being brought to trial. The title indicates that witchcraft is a significant focus in the play, but modern feminist readers in search of oppressed sisters need to look elsewhere.[20]

The reality of sixteenth- and seventeenth-century witch-hunts was that they were likely to victimise women who were old, poor and unmarried (especially widowed) and who grumbled or cursed in response to hardship. Hecate and her cohorts, however, do not fit these categories. Hecate, although mortal and clearly not a goddess, really does fly, run a coven, have familiars, cast spells, cook dead babies and all the things witches were supposed to do,[21] but there is an absurd element to her: for example her use of standard charlatan tricks in I.ii or her almost jolly attitude towards evil doing. This can be contrasted with the witch-charac-

---

see Sir John Harington's account of the festivities in July 1606 for a visit by Christian IV of Denmark in *Nugae Antiquae* (1804, reprinted 1966), pp. 348–53.

[19] Standard works on the witch hunts include Alan Macfarlane, *Witchcraft in Tudor and Stuart England: A Regional and Comparative Study* (1970) and Keith Thomas, *Religion and the Decline of Magic* (1971). See also Christina Larner, *The Enemies of God* (1983) and *Witchcraft and Religion* (1984) and Barbara Ehrenreich and Deirdre English, *Witches, Midwives and Nurses: A History of Women Healers* (1976). A feminist and deliberately iconoclastic critique of Thomas and Macfarlane is offered by Marianne Hester in *Lewd Women and Wicked Witches: A Study of the Dynamics of Male Domination* (1992).

[20] E.g. the socialist feminist account of the witch-hunts in Caryl Churchill's play *Vinegar Tom* and the more radical feminist account in Sarah Daniels's play *Byrthrite*. See also Kathleen McLuskie's comments in her *Renaissance Dramatists* (1989), p. 60.

[21] *The Witch* displays witch practices (covens, flying etc.) that used to be seen as more typical of continental European than English belief, the latter usually being characterised as revolving around simple maleficium or casting a spell of misfortune on someone.

ter Mother Sawyer in *The Witch of Edmonton*. Mother Sawyer is at first presented sympathetically and credibly: the play begins by offering a convincing picture of how a disempowered old woman desires to become a witch in order to retaliate against her enemies. The fact that the play then shows the old woman successfully becoming a malicious and powerful witch – one able to cause death – confirms the stereotype that old woman equals witch, a stereotype that could affect the lives of real old women, living in every village, vulnerable to attack.[22] By contrast Middleton presents a fantastic, and I believe tongue-in-cheek, caricature of witches.

The witch scenes in the play are also challenging because they present the witches as less obnoxious than the human characters. The comparison is clearly invited by the parallelism of the two opening scenes (see pp. xxvii–xxviii). Sometimes the witch scenes seem irrelevant to the main action except for the fact that the witches provide almost a local shop, casually used by the court whenever a poison or potion is required. However, Middleton's witches also provide a compelling focus for a subject that Middleton often explored in his plays: his society's neurosis about female chastity.

Hecate and her witches have little time for chastity, and they roam around at night picking out delicious young men. If nothing promising turns up Hecate will make do with her son, Firestone, or even the cat, Malkin, rather than go without sex. However, while the witches' cheerful promiscuity is certainly condemned by the play, abiding by society's norms for female sexuality and the cult of female chastity is shown as almost equally repulsive. Three plot lines are dominated by the question of female chastity: Francisca turns to murder by proxy in order to hide her loss of virginity; the duchess is willing to be executed as a murderer but fights to clear her name of the sin of unchastity, which to her is worse than murder; and the technicality of who is to break Isabella's hymen absorbs the energies of Antonio, Sebastian and his friend, Fernando. Sebastian in particular goes to absurd lengths, obtaining a spell from Hecate in order to secure his 'rights' in relation to Isabella's hymen and to prevent Antonio from usurping that 'right'. What initially appears to be extremism in Francisca's behaviour later appears to be commonsensical when we see her brother's reaction to her confession that she has lost her virginity: Antonio goes berserk and deems death the only appropriate reward for the man and woman who have thus disgraced his family name. Antonio's behaviour (which, given

[22] See Peter Stallybrass, '*Macbeth* and Witchcraft', in *Focus on 'Macbeth'*, ed. John Russell Brown (1982), p. 206.

his relationship with Florida, is crassly hypocritical) makes Francisca's deceptions seem sensible rather than callous.

Maintaining a reputation for impeccable chastity is an urgent problem for most of the women characters in *The Witch*, just as it is for real women in any patriarchal society. Middleton offers almost a survey of the possible roles available to women – wife, bride, unmarried mother, prostitute, witch – and all except Florida and Hecate are fighting to keep their reputations intact. The range of roles under discussion is emphasised by Isabella's song in II.i, which assesses the comparative merits of the states of maid, wife and widow. Because of the pressure to maintain their reputations (deserved or not), when women want to strike at one another they know exactly where other women's point of maximum vulnerability is. Both Francisca and Florida try to discredit Isabella's claim to chastity, since without it Isabella's status in her society will be destroyed. The hypocrisy of the men in relation to female chastity is also baldly demonstrated in the play. Not only is Antonio's hypocrisy almost laughably blatant, but also Almachildes (III.i) complains that the woman he thought to deflower did not have an intact hymen and so had deceived him. Sebastian claims a heavenly union with Isabella but comes close to raping her, asserting self-righteously that it is his right so to do.

Middleton's concern with the dangerous absurdities to which an obsession about female chastity leads is one of the many points of contact between *The Witch* and his later play (with Rowley) *The Changeling*.[23] Like Francisca, Beatrice-Joanna in *The Changeling* is prepared to murder to conceal the loss of her virginity, and this results in an uneasy mix of tragedy and farce. Francisca's plot to disgrace and discredit her sister-in-law evolves into a murder plot characterised by a confused sequence of entrances and exits that begins to resemble a bedroom farce. Beatrice-Joanna is subjected to a virginity-test where the symptoms of true virginity (sneezing, laughing and yawning) are absurd. This quality is reinforced by the fact that the ridiculous symptoms are performed twice, first by Diaphanta, and then by Beatrice-Joanna. The test is utterly worthless because it can be so easily faked, but as a symptom of patriarchal neurosis it is extremely significant. Beatrice-Joanna has learned from her patriarchal culture that to lose her reputation for chastity would be so appalling that murder is preferable. Consequently, like the duchess in *The Witch* (V.iii.101–2), Beatrice-Joanna is more willing to confess publicly to murder than to unchastity. This

[23] See note 13. Heinemann, *Puritanism and Theatre*, p. 111, suggests that 'Francisca . . . seems like a first sketch for Beatrice-Joanna'.

distorted morality is particularly emphasised in *The Witch* as there is so much hullabaloo over which woman precisely Almachildes has penetrated: first it seems that it may be Amoretta, then that it may be the duchess and finally it turns out that it was a common prostitute. A bitter comedy emerges, focussed around the grotesque comic device of the bed trick, where one woman is substituted for another without the man concerned noticing the difference. Middleton also uses bed tricks in *A Game at Chess* and *The Changeling*. In a play where the focus on female chastity and sex is so strong (this is true also of Shakespeare's bed tricks in *Measure for Measure* and *All's Well That Ends Well*), the bed trick points uncomfortably to the utter reification of women in the act of sex, as each woman becomes an anonymous body to be penetrated, not an individual with distinguishing marks.[24]

The Witch also connects with *The Changeling* in several plot devices. Both plays show a woman (Amoretta, Beatrice-Joanna) manipulating a man who lusts after her (Almachildes, De Flores). Both plays counterpoint the main action with a sub-plot concerning a society that seems alien but turns out to be in fact very much in tune with the protagonists (the witches' coven, the madhouse). Both plays show women (the duchess, Beatrice-Joanna) attempting to be Machiavellian but failing rather pathetically. Both plays show passion as deadly – a bewitching or a madness; both also deal in sensational stage properties (the skull, the finger) as well as referring to the same court scandal, the Essex divorce and the murder of Overbury.

The topical satire in *The Witch* is important from a critical point of view. If the play is seen primarily as a topical satire, as a seventeenth-century equivalent of *Spitting Image*, some of the supposed 'problems' of the play seem less urgent. Nothing dates more quickly than topical satire, which depends very much on the audience identifying targets and concentrating on how these targets are represented. Topical satire also needs no compelling narrative line (as is shown by *A Game at Chess*), so the fact that in *The Witch* the plot line sometimes hardly makes sense is of little significance. Consider Sebastian's machinations in IV.ii, which are deeply confusing. The best sense that can be made of them is that Sebastian has plotted that Florida will meet Isabella at Fernando's house and that Florida will lay claim to Antonio in some way (this is based on Isabella's comments at IV.ii.74–5,

[24] Bed tricks used by male Renaissance dramatists generally have the woman deceiving the man, and the trick works. By contrast the Restoration dramatist Aphra Behn in *The Lucky Chance* rewrites and reverses the device of the bed trick: the woman to be deceived realises what is happening and prevents it.

81–2, although this theory partly depends on an emendation to IV.ii.27). Isabella also expects to find Antonio at Fernando's house, but clearly Sebastian cannot arrange for this to happen. Florida thinks she is taking part in a plot to disgrace Isabella in Antonio's eyes, because Isabella will be caught out of her own house at night in the company of 'Celio' and so disgraced. Florida also believes she is going to have a night with Antonio. Sebastian presumably hopes that Isabella, enraged by the evidence that her husband is unfaithful, will be slightly easier to seduce or rape. Sebastian is going to rape Isabella, on the grounds that this is his lawful right because of their precontract, but then he has a change of heart. What Sebastian laughably calls his 'plain' plot then gets enmeshed with Francisca's plot to discredit Isabella, and the confusion is compounded. No-one can follow this narrative in the theatre, but if the emphasis of the play is on ridiculing recognisable targets of personal satire, the need for Middleton's audience to follow the plot, as opposed to laughing at the characters' confusion, would have been less urgent. Plots do not always make clear sense in Middleton (for example the end of the Antonio plot in *The Changeling*), but Sebastian's convoluted plotting really suggests that clarity of narrative is not the dramatist's priority here.

In *The Witch* great 'folks' get away with murder and it is expected that high rank will allow sinners to go unpunished (e.g. IV.i.51–3, V.i.93–4). Not only is it evident in the play that the witches will not be caught and tried but there is also no question of any character being punished for using the witches' services or attempting criminal acts. The duchess is pardoned, Sebastian gets his Isabella, Almachildes is merely exposed as a fool. Only Antonio falls down a hole into hell, and he was one of the few characters who did not use the witches.[25] These formal happy endings may appear qualified, but the fact that many of the characters have avoided punishment for misdeeds committed, or intended, is important and complements the emphasis on characters attempting to 'rid' themselves of evidence of misdoing (e.g. I.i.38, II.iii.9, 14: the duchess attempting to rid herself of Almachildes; Aberzanes and Francisca ridding themselves of their baby). An alternative to avoiding punishment is of course repentance, but when this option is mentioned (e.g. the duke in V.iii, Antonio in relation to Aberzanes and Francisca), the morally dubious status of the character who is recommending repentance totally undercuts the idea.

The Witch has not received a great deal of critical scrutiny in comparison with the more popular Middleton plays such as *The*

[25] Anne Lancashire, '*The Witch*: Stage Flop or Political Mistake?', pp. 172–3

Changeling and *Women Beware Women*; it has been discussed as a tragicomedy, as a parody of Beaumont and Fletcher, as the 'middle of Middleton', as a theatrical failure.[26] My emphasis would be that *The Witch* clearly anticipates *The Changeling* and also *Women Beware Women* in its presentation of women characters as being distorted by their culture into practising internecine warfare and immorality. The Revels editors (p. 19) also find in *The Witch* 'an all-pervasive irony' that anticipates these two later plays. The opening banquet scene of *The Witch*, in particular, looks forward to the central banquet scene of *Women Beware Women* (III.iii) in its complex structure and carefully paced relaying of plot information and development. I would also stress the link between the endings of *The Witch* and *Women Beware Women*. Both are uncompromising and astonishing. In *The Witch* the ludicrous ending also ensures that most questions raised by the play are left unanswered despite (indeed because of?) the absurdly superficial neatness of the ending.

STAGING AND STAGE HISTORY

The text is at least one remove from playhouse practice, as is clear from its failure to indicate several necessary entrances and exits. The manuscript title-page tells us the play was 'acted, by his Majesty's Servants at the Blackfriars', and Lancashire (pp. 162–3) is right to caution us against reading the phrase 'ill fated' as meaning 'failed in the playhouse', because it could equally be interpreted as 'censored off stage', or 'suppressed'. Thomas Holmes's interest in the play certainly makes more sense if it was suppressed because of scandal rather than being a box office failure. However, we know nothing about the premiere performance(s) of *The Witch* apart from the fact that it/they took place at Blackfriars.

Blackfriars was an indoor playhouse with a smaller stage than the outdoor playhouses and with more capacity for impressive scenic and some lighting effects.[27] It is likely that the witch scenes would have been staged with considerable spectacle. Because of the more reliable acoustics in the indoor playhouses, music was often a feature of performances, and this again would be

[26] See, e.g., John F. McElroy, *Parody and Burlesque in the Tragicomedies of Thomas Middleton* (1972); Samuel Schoenbaum, 'Middleton's Tragi-comedies', *Modern Philology* 54 (1956), 7–19; Inga-Stina Ewbank, 'The Middle of Middleton'.

[27] Gurr, *The Shakespearean Stage*, pp. 143–7. Glynne Wickham discusses staging possibilities in relation to sections of *The Witch* that appear in *Macbeth* in 'To Fly or Not to Fly? The Problem of Hecate in Shakespeare's *Macbeth*', in *Essays on Drama and Theatre* (1973).

important in the witch scenes. The other main staging requirement of the play is a two-level playing area for IV.iii.

Jonson's *Masque of Queens* gives some idea of how spectacular a performance of *The Witch* could have been. Jonson's masque was performed at court with no expense spared (Frances, then Countess of Essex, participated in it); and while the commercial theatre company, the King's Men, would not have been so extravagant, the description of the court masque costume and dancing is still suggestive of what could be achieved. Jonson describes his witches thus: 'some, with rats on their heads; some, on their shoulders; others with ointment-pots at their girdles; all with spindles, timbrels, rattles or other venefical instruments, making a confused noise, with strange gestures'. When the Dame enters she is 'naked armed, bare footed, her frock tucked, her hair knotted, and folded with vipers; in her hand a torch made of a dead man's arm, lighted; girded with a snake' (p. 286). Jonson describes the witches' dance as follows: 'full of preposterous change, and gesticulation, . . . all things contrary to the custom of men, dancing, back to back, hip to hip, their hands joined, and making their circles backward, to the left hand, with strange fantastic motions of their heads, and bodies' (p. 301).

In the twentieth century *The Witch* has not been acted professionally, but there have been enterprising student productions. In 1986, Robert Jones directed the play for Warwick University Dramatic Society.[28] In 1988 (July 7–9, 12–16) Ormond College dramatic society at the University of Melbourne presented the play in the Union theatre. This production, directed by Mark Williams, billed the play as 'a hilarious four-plot tragi-comedy, with witches'.[29] There has also been a production of the play at Queen's University, Kingston, Canada.

Although *The Witch* does not have a recorded professional stage history, the scenes it shares with *Macbeth* have been professionally produced. For a long time after the Restoration productions of *Macbeth*, in particular those based around Davenant's adaptation, took their cue from the scenes shared with *The Witch* and produced witches with an emphasis on singing, dancing and sometimes comedy. With a return to high seriousness in productions of *Macbeth* in the nineteenth and twentieth centuries, Hecate and her cohorts tended to be banished from the stage. Two particularly notable exceptions to this tendency are Frank Dunlop's production at the Young Vic in 1975 and Peter Hall and John Russell Brown's production at the National

[28] For a review of this production see *Research Opportunities in Renaissance Drama* 29 (1986–7), 63.

[29] Information provided by Ken Woodgate, Melbourne

Theatre in 1978. Dunlop's production made *Macbeth* into the witches' play, many felt at the expense of Macbeth's tragic status as he became the witches' puppet. Hecate and her coven opened and closed the play 'invoking the dark gods up and down the Young Vic aisles' (Michael Billington in *The Guardian*, 16 January 1975). The National Theatre production was more restrained in its use of the witches, but some critics disapproved of its beautiful young Hecate (clearly not Middleton's witch). In general, critical response to the inclusion of the Hecate material in both these productions was disapproving and suggested that the critics concerned had very set and conservative conceptions of the effect that the witches are supposed to achieve in *Macbeth*.

The witch scenes in *The Witch*, judging from the University of Melbourne production, constitute one of the strongest aspects of the play. They are entertaining and visually impressive, and there is a powerful dramatic tension produced by the juxtaposition of the wild, fantastic and funny witch scenes with the moody, troubled and murderous court scenes. The witch scenes tend to upstage the court scenes and mock them; they also contrast in pace with most of the court scenes, which are packed with narrative. In addition a broadly comic reading of the witches' scenes helps highlight the comic element present in the gruesome horror in some of the court scenes.

One of the most crucial production questions raised by *The Witch* (and also by *Macbeth*) is how the witches are to be represented on-stage. In *The Witch* (I.ii.119–20) Sebastian seems to suggest that Hecate's appearance is fearful and horrific, and she is called 'hag' (ll. 178, 198) and 'foul' (III.iii.17). Similarly *Macbeth*'s witches are described in terms that suggest the haggish: they have beards; they are 'withered' and 'wild' in their attire; they have skinny lips and choppy fingers (*Macbeth* I.iii.40, 44–6). Jonson's description of the witches from *Masque of Queens* suggests a more emblematically evil appearance, but there is a dignity to these descriptions that is a long way from Hecate and Firestone's double act and even knockabout humour (e.g. the end of I.ii). Firestone is present in the witch scenes primarily to point the audience in the direction of the comic.

There are problems in staging witches as hags in the late twentieth century. Feminist analysis would want to dispute the stereotype. Film realism has introduced new standards in the horrific, and audiences are less likely to be impressed by stereotype hags. The most readily available twentieth-century images of witches are not frightening: hags evoke Hammer House of Horror, fairy tales and radical feminists who claim to be revolting hags. The lack of terror is sometimes perceived to be a problem in relation to staging *Macbeth*, but it is a bonus in *The Witch*, where the hags are far more fun than terrifying.

Inga-Stina Ewbank speculates over how much the original performances of *The Witch* played on an audience's experience of seeing the same performers play in *Macbeth*.[30] There is also the question of whether the original performance of *The Witch* included a deliberate parody of *Macbeth*; this may be suggested by the large number of echoes of *Macbeth* in *The Witch*. I see these echoes working rather like the echoes of *Hamlet* in *The Revenger's Tragedy*, mocking the earlier work. This could be a strength in performance: although it would be impossible to play *The Witch* now so that the audience could pick up on the Howard/Carr/Essex satire, it would be possible to play it as a satire of *Macbeth*, and to perform the two plays alongside each other would give *The Witch* real bite: for example, the basic impulse in all of the major narratives in *The Witch* is to go to the witches to effect some skullduggery, and the equanimity with which so many characters do this could be used to parody the agonisings of Macbeth over his encounters with witches.

There are no star parts in *The Witch* and no character that the audience can strongly identify with. The play condemns a corrupt society rather than focusing on one or two individuals. This can make *The Witch* appear 'difficult' for students and performers inculcated with the ideal of strong and convincing characterisation, as is often found in Shakespeare but less commonly in, for example, Jonson and Middleton. Shakespeare's dominance in the repertory has been partially responsible for the emphasis on characterisation in British theatre, but *The Witch* clearly and deliberately takes a different path. However, because of the crowded narrative, characters need to be strongly individualised, for example by gesture and costume.

For the late twentieth-century theatre-goer perhaps the most stageworthy aspect of *The Witch* is its Ortonesque black humour. Another strength is the extraordinary and disconcerting swings in mood – from broad farce (Almachildes and the witches) to deadpan (the ending), from mordant humour (the callousness of Francisca's plotting) to casual murder. This pattern of extraordinary swings in mood is set particularly effectively in the opening two scenes of the play.

The first scene presents the audience with an enormous amount of information very quickly and covers a wide variety of theatrical genres. All the main plot lines are introduced, family relationships established and recent histories recounted; we pass from romantic tragedy with Sebastian, through citizen comedy

[30] 'The Middle of Middleton', p. 157

intrigue with Florida, to romantic comedy verging on broad comedy with Almachildes and Amoretta. Finally we have the shock of the duke's use of his father-in-law's skull, compounded by the suddenness with which he produces it. That some sort of sensational reaction is produced on-stage is suggested by the duke's comment 'Fie, how you fright the women!' (I.i.111). This is a very uneasy, perverse moment, wavering between farce and horror. But however this final part of the first scene is played, the second scene parallels and undercuts it: another banquet is presented, and the witches' ingredients are as bizarre as the duke's use of the skull. The duke's action is thus closely allied to the fantastic and ridiculous world of Hecate and Firestone, something which could be easily reinforced by blocking – placing the leader of the coven, Hecate, where the leader of the court, the duke, has just been standing to reinforce their shared taste in gruesome stage properties.

The second scene also moves gradually closer to farce: Firestone's presence encourages us to look for the comic even in Sebastian's melodramatic posturing, but when Almachildes is introduced with farcical tumbling and a rather sadly unambitious request for an aphrodisiac charm, the tone is clearly comic. The swings in mood from the beginning of the act to the end are thus enormous. Similarly extreme changes in mood also appear elsewhere; for example, the farce of Almachildes' narrative in its early stages is transformed as he becomes entangled in a serious murder plot, which is then undercut by the ludicrous ending. Playing on these surprising swings in mood, on the black comedy and the satire of the immoral casualness towards murder that prevails in the court scenes would be to play to *The Witch*'s strengths.

THE TEXT

The manuscript of *The Witch* is in the Bodleian Library at Oxford (MS Malone 12). The scribe who produced the manuscript, Ralph Crane, has been thoroughly studied, particularly in relation to his contribution to the production of the Shakespeare First Folio.[31] Crane was a professional scrivener, and it seems

[31] E.g. F. P. Wilson, 'Ralph Crane, Scrivener to the King's Players', *The Library* 7 (1926), 194–215; W. W. Greg, 'Some Notes on Crane's Manuscript of *The Witch*', *The Library* 22 (1942), 208–22; T. H. Howard-Hill, 'Shakespeare's Earliest Editor, Ralph Crane', *Shakespeare Survey* 44 (1992), 113–29; *'A Game at Chess' by Thomas Middleton: A Textual Edition Based on the Manuscripts Written by Ralph Crane*, ed. Milton Arthur Buettner (1980).

reasonable to trust his work to a large extent. However, he had many idiosyncracies: he loved colons and semi-colons; his question marks and exclamation marks are often indistinguishable; he used brackets enthusiastically, especially around titles and vocatives; he liked stringing adjectives and nouns together with hyphens. To follow his heavy and idiosyncratic punctuation (especially when we know Middleton's punctuation was light) would be confusing for most modern readers, and so this text of *The Witch* has been punctuated lightly, with the aim of making sense even when the text itself does not.

Crane edited as well as transcribed – he may well have edited out some profanity as he did in other texts – but it is largely impossible to conjecture what he may have changed or misread. When we compare a Crane transcript with a Middleton manuscript of *A Game at Chess*, patterns in Crane's alterations (usually expansions) of Middleton's favourite elisions appear. However, this edition follows Crane's elisions most of the time and modernises elisions such as 'h'as' (I.i.40, 41) for clarity. Crane also occasionally uses elision to mark the omission of a word such as 'the' or 'is'.

Crane often marks entries early, but some entries and exits he does not mark at all. I have altered stage entrances and exits wherever it seems appropriate.

It is often difficult to tell whether Crane is representing verse or prose: prose lines are not written out as markedly longer than verse lines, and he does not capitalise the first word of a verse line. This problem is compounded by Middleton's flexible verse forms, which make the distinction between the two unclear. Certain characters (Firestone, Almachildes) seem to use prose more frequently, but many of the verse/prose distinctions in this edition are not meant to be categorical.

The Witch was first printed by Isaac Reed in 1778. It has been edited several times since, and several new editions are about to be published. The nineteenth-century editions tend to punctuate very heavily and to regularise the verse lines over-enthusiastically.

In this edition spelling has been modernised, abbreviations have been expanded and substantive changes to the copy text have been recorded in the notes. Spelling has also been modernised in the quotations from Scot and Jonson.

Al. And I the last man then: I may deserve
to be first one day.

Gou. Sir, it has gon round now.

Du. The round! an excellent way to trayne-up Soldiers.
where's Bride, and Bride-groome.

An. At your happie service.

Du. A Boy to night at least: I charge you looke to't
or I'll renounce you for industrious Subiects.

An. your Grace speakes like a worthy, and tryde Soldier. —Ext.

Gasp. And you'll doe well, for one that nere tost-pike (Sir) —Exit

Scen. 2a. Enter Heccat: & other witches: (with Properties, and Habitts fitting.)

Hec. Titty, and Tiffin, Suckin
and Pidgin, Liard, and Robin
white Spiritts, black Spiritts, gray Spiritts: red Spiritts:
Devill-Toad, Devill-Ram: Devill-Catt: and Devill Dam.
why Hoppo, and Stadlin, Hellwin, & Prickle.

Stad. here, sweating at the Vessell.

Hec. Boyle it well.

Hop. it gallops now.

Hec. Are the flames blew enough?
or shall I vse a litle seething more?

Stad. the Nipps of Fayries vpon Maides white hipps
are not more perfect Azure.

Tend

The Bodleian Library, Oxford, MS Malone 12

Hec. Tend it carefully,
Send Stadlin to me with a Brazen dish
that I may fall to work vpon these Serpents,
and squiez'd em ready for the second howre.
why when.

Stad. Heere's Stadlin, and the dish.

Hec. there take this vn-baptized Brat:
Boile it well; preserve the fat,
you know 'tis pretious to transfer
our 'noynted flesh into the Aire
in Moone-light nights, on Steeple-Topps,
Mountaines, and pine-trees, that like pricks, or Stopps,
seeme to our height: high Towres, and Roofes of Princes
like wrinckles in the Earth: whole Provinces
appeare to our sight then, ev'n leeke
a russet-Moale, vpon some Ladies cheeke.
when hundred leagues in Aire, we feast, and sing,
daunce, kisse, and coll, vse every thing;
what young-man can we wish, to pleasure vs
but we enioy him in an Incubus?
thou know'st it Stadlin?

Sta. vsually that's don.

Hec. Last night thou got'st the Maior of Whelplies Son
I knew him by his black Cloake lyn'd with yellow,
I thinck thou'hast spoild the youth: hee's but seaventeene.
I'll haue him the next Mounting: away in.

Go.

FURTHER READING

A. A. Bromham, 'The Date of *The Witch* and the Essex Divorce Case', *NQ* 225 (1980), 149–52

A. A. Bromham and Zara Bruzzi, *'The Changeling' and the Years of Crisis, 1619–24* (1990)

Peter Corbin and Douglas Sedge, eds., *Three Jacobean Witchcraft Plays*, Revels Plays Companion Library (1986)

Inga-Stina Ewbank, 'The Middle of Middleton', in *The Arts of Performance in Elizabethan and Early Stuart Drama: Essays for G. K. Hunter*, ed. Murray Biggs et al. (1991)

Margot Heinemann, *Puritanism and Theatre: Thomas Middleton and Opposition Drama under the Early Stuarts* (1980)

Anne Lancashire, '*The Witch*: Stage Flop or Political Mistake?' in '*Accompaninge the Players', Essays in Celebration of Thomas Middleton, 1580–1980*, ed. Kenneth Friedenreich (1983)

John F. McElroy, *Parody and Burlesque in the Tragicomedies of Thomas Middleton* (1972)

Keith Thomas, *Religion and the Decline of Magic* (1971)

Beatrice White, *Cast of Ravens: The Strange Case of Sir Thomas Overbury* (1965)

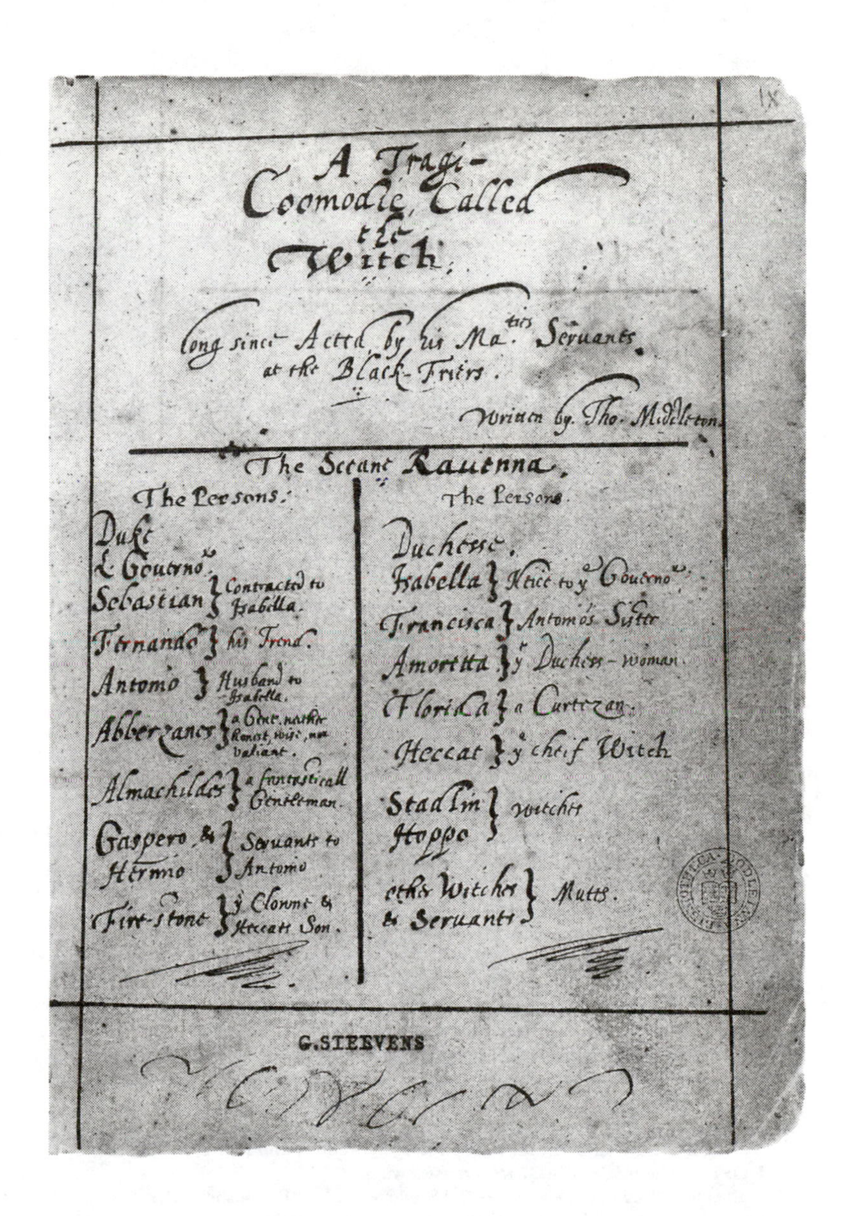

A Tragi-
Coomodie, Called
the
Witch.

long since Acted by his Maties Seruants
at the Black-Friers.

Written by. Tho. Middleton.

The Sceane Rauenna.

The Persons.

Duke
L. Gouerno.^r^
Sebastian } Contracted to Isabella.
Fernando } his Frend.
Antonio } Husband to Isabella.
Aberzanes } a Gent. neither honest, wise, nor valiant.
Almachildes } a fantasticall Gentleman.
Gaspero & Hermio } Seruants to Antonio
Firestone } ye Clowne & Heccats Son.

The Persons.

Duchesse.
Isabella } Neice to ye Gouerno.^r^
Francisca } Antonio's Sister
Amoretta } ye Duches-woman.
Florida } a Curtezan.
Heccat } ye cheif Witch
Stadlin, Hoppo } witches
other Witches & Seruants } Mutes.

The Bodleian Library, Oxford, MS Malone 12, title page

2–3 *Long . . . Blackfriars* See Introduction, p. xxiv.
5 *Ravenna* a token location given the details of London life, the use of a Scottish accent in II.i and the MS reference to Urbin at V.iii.54
13 *fantastical* foppish in attire
14 GASPERO sometimes called Gasper
17 DUCHESS called Rosamund in Machiavelli but here called Amoretta so that the joke of II.ii will work
19 FRANCISCA a common name for prostitutes (especially in the form 'Frank' or 'Frankie' because of its suggestion of giving sexual favours frankly); also a name suggestive of Frances Carr (see Introduction, p. xvi)
22 HECATE two syllables, as the MS spelling is 'Heccat'. In Greek mythology Hecate is goddess of the moon and witchcraft. This Hecate, however, is not a goddess as she is expecting to die when she is 120 years old (see I.ii.68).
23–4 STADLIN, HOPPO See Scot 12.5: 'It is constantly affirmed in M.MAL. that STAFUS used always to hide himself in a mousehole, and had a disciple called HOPPO, who made STADLIN a master witch'.
25–6 HELLWAIN *and* PUCKLE See Scot 7.15, where the list of spirits includes 'the hell wain . . . the puckle'. Puckle is not entirely mute in this edition as I have attributed III.iii.45–8 to her.
27 MALKIN diminutive of Matilda or Maud, although I.ii.95–6 suggests the 'great cat' is male

[DRAMATIS PERSONAE]

A Tragi-Comedy, called 'The Witch'

Long since acted by his Majesty's Servants
at the Blackfriars,
written by Thomas Middleton.

The scene Ravenna 5

THE PERSONS
DUKE
LORD GOVERNOR
SEBASTIAN, contracted to Isabella
FERNANDO, his friend 10
ANTONIO, husband to Isabella
ABERZANES, a gentleman neither honest, wise nor valiant
ALMACHILDES, a fantastical gentleman
GASPERO }
HERMIO } servants to Antonio 15
FIRESTONE, the clown and Hecate's son

DUCHESS
ISABELLA, niece to the Lord Governor
FRANCISCA, Antonio's sister
AMORETTA, the Duchess' woman 20
FLORIDA, a courtesan
HECATE, the chief witch
STADLIN }
HOPPO } witches
Other witches [including HELLWAIN and } 25
PUCKLE] & servants } mutes
[MALKIN] a spirit like a cat
[A boy]
[An old woman]
[Messengers, attendants on the Lord Governor] 30

To the truly worthy and generously affected
Thomas Holmes, Esquire

Noble Sir,
As a true testimony of my ready inclination to your service, I have, merely upon a taste of your desire, recovered into 5
my hands (though not without much difficulty) this ignorantly ill-fated labour of mine. Witches are, *ipso facto*, by the law condemned and that only, I think, hath made her lie so long in an imprisoned obscurity. For your sake alone she hath thus far conjured herself abroad and bears no other 10
charms about her but what may tend to your recreation, nor no other spell but to possess you with a belief that as she, so he that first taught her to enchant, will always be, your devoted
Tho[mas] Middleton. 15

2 *Thomas Holmes, Esquire* Wayne Phelps, 'Thomas Holmes, Esquire: The Dedicatee of Middleton's *The Witch*', *NQ* 27 (1980), 152–4, argues that the title 'Esquire' indicates that the dedicatee could not be a clergyman, and this eliminates all known possible dedicatees except for a Thomas Holmes of Gray's Inn. Phelps dismisses the previous favourite, Thomas Holmes the composer (lay-vicar of Winchester 1631, gentleman of the Chapel Royal 1633, died 1638), on the 'Esquire' test and because he flourished too late for contact with Middleton; however, Grove dates Holmes's birth date as around 1580, which would make him the same age as Middleton. What we know of Holmes of Winchester – e.g. that he sang bass in a masque by Shirley in 1633 – also suggests that he would be interested in *The Witch*. If Holmes's interest in *The Witch* was expressed around 1624, he may not have been ordained then, and so even Phelps's 'Esquire' test is unconvincing.

6–7 *ignorantly ill-fated* not necessarily a stage flop (see Introduction, pp. xiv, xxiv)

9 *imprisoned obscurity* The play text probably had to be retrieved from the King's Men, who would own the text once they had bought it from Middleton.

10 *conjured herself abroad* i.e. gone abroad in the form of the manuscript

THE WITCH

Act I, Scene i

Enter SEBASTIAN *and* FERNANDO

SEBASTIAN
My three years spent in war has now undone
My peace for ever.
FERNANDO Good, be patient sir.
SEBASTIAN
She is my wife by contract before heaven
And all the angels sir.
FERNANDO I do believe you,
But where's the remedy now? You see she's gone; 5
Another has possession.
SEBASTIAN There's the torment.
FERNANDO
This day being the first of your return
Unluckily proves the first too of her fastening.
Her uncle, sir, the governor of Ravenna,
Holding a good opinion of the bridegroom, 10
As he's fair spoken, sir, and wondrous mild –
SEBASTIAN
There goes the devil in a sheepskin!
FERNANDO – with all speed
Clapped it up suddenly. I cannot think, sure,
That the maid over-loves him – though being married
Perhaps, for her own credit, now she intends 15
Performance of an honest, duteous wife.

0 MS uses Latin act and scene terminology throughout the text and marks the end of each act in Latin.
3 *She* Isabella
3–4 They had a verbal marriage contract but had not consummated it; therefore it was not legally recognised. Fernando witnessed the verbal contract (see IV.ii.4–5), and Sebastian's belief in its legality determines his behaviour in the play.
6 *possession* Once the marriage is consummated it will have legal standing.
8 *fastening* i.e. marriage
12 *There ... sheep-skin!* The bridegroom (Antonio) is a devil (wolf) in sheep's clothing.
13 *Clapped it up* settled it
14 *over-loves* loves him especially strongly
15 *credit* reputation 16 *Performance of* to fulfil her duty as

SEBASTIAN
Sir, I've a world of business. Question nothing;
You will but lose your labour; 'tis not fit
For any – hardly mine own secrecy –
To know what I intend. I take my leave sir. 20
I find such strange employments in myself
That unless death pity me, and lay me down,
I shall not sleep these seven years; that's the least sir.

Exit

FERNANDO
That sorrow's dangerous can abide no counsel;
'Tis like a wound past cure. Wrongs done to love 25
Strike the heart deeply; none can truly judge on't
But the poor, sensible sufferer whom it racks
With unbelieved pains, which men in health,
That enjoy love, not possibly can act –
Nay, not so much as think. In troth, I pity him; 30
His sighs drink life-blood in this time of feasting.

[*Sound of banquet within*]

A banquet towards too? Not yet hath riot
Played out her last scene? At such entertainments still
Forgetfulness obeys and surfeit governs.
Here's marriage sweetly honoured in gorged stomachs 35
And overflowing cups!

Enter GASPERO *and* SERVANT

GASPERO [*To* SERVANT] Where is she sirrah?
SERVANT
Not far off.
GASPERO Prithee where? Go fetch her hither.

[*Exit* SERVANT]

19 *hardly my own secrecy* even my own secret thoughts
21 *employments* preoccupations 23 *that's the least* at the very least
24 *can* that can 27 *sensible* sensitive, feeling
28 *unbelieved* unbelievable
29 *act* act out, experience and so understand
31 *sighs . . . life-blood* Sighing was believed to emit vital spirits and so in excess could be life threatening. Cf. *A Midsummer Night's Dream* III.ii.97.
s.d. *banquet* after-dinner wine and sweets
32 *towards* about to take place
32–3 *Not . . . scene?* i.e. hasn't the debauched revelry finished yet?
34 *obeys* is obeyed, is dominant
surfeit excess, gluttony, drunkenness and sexual promiscuity

I'll rid him away straight.
[*To* FERNANDO] The duke's now risen sir.

FERNANDO
I am a joyful man to hear it sir;
It seems he's drunk the less – though I think he 40
That has the least he's certainly enough. *Exit*

GASPERO
I have observed this fellow; all the feast-time
He hath not pledged one cup, but looked most wickedly
Upon good Malego, flies to the black-jack still
And sticks to small drink like a water-rat. 45

Enter FLORIDA

Oh here she comes. Alas, the poor whore weeps.
'Tis not for grace now, all the world must judge;
It is for spleen and madness 'gainst this marriage.
I do but think how she could beat the vicar now,
Scratch the man horribly that gave the woman, 50
The woman worst of all, if she durst do it.
[*To* FLORIDA] Why how now mistress? This weeping needs not; for though
My master marry for his reputation,
He means to keep you too.

FLORIDA How sir?

GASPERO He doth indeed;
He swore't to me last night. Are you so simple, 55
And have been five years traded, as to think
One woman would serve him? Fie, not an empress!
Why he'll be sick o'th' wife within ten nights
Or never trust my judgement.

FLORIDA Will he, think'st thou?

GASPERO
Will he!

FLORIDA I find thee still so comfortable – 60
Beshrew my heart if I know how to miss thee.

38 *rid him* get rid of Fernando
duke's ed. (King's MS)
44 *Malego* white wine exported from Malaga
black-jack large leather jug for beer
44–5 i.e. he avoids wine and sticks to low alcohol 'small beer'
47 *not for grace* i.e. not in penitence, which would bring her to grace
48 *spleen* fit of temper, passion
56 *traded* sold, prostituted
60 *comfortable* comforting
61 *know* ed. (knew MS)
to miss manage without

They talk of gentlemen, perfumers and such things;
Give me the kindness of the master's man
In my distress, say I.

GASPERO 'Tis your great love, forsooth.
Please you withdraw yourself to yond private parlour. 65
I'll send you ven'son, custard, parsnip pie.
For banquetting stuff – as suckets, jellies, syrups –
I will bring in myself.

FLORIDA I'll take 'em kindly sir. *Exit*

GASPERO
She's your grand strumpet's complement to a tittle.
'Tis a fair building; it had need; it has 70
Just at this time some one and twenty inmates –
But half of 'em are young merchants; they'll depart
shortly –
They take but rooms for summer and away they
When't grows foul weather. Marry, then come the
termers
And commonly they're well booted for all seasons. 75

Enter ALMACHILDES *and* AMORETTA

But peace, no more; the guests are coming in.
[GASPERO *retires*]

ALMACHILDES
The fates have blessed me. Have I met you privately?

[*Attempts to kiss* AMORETTA]

AMORETTA
Why sir! Why Almachildes!

ALMACHILDES Not a kiss?

63 *master's man* servant
66 *ven'son* venison
custard made of eggs and milk but not necessarily sweet, as in quiche
67 *suckets* fruit preserved in sugar
69 *complement* full number of personal accomplishments
to a tittle with minute exactness
70 *it had need* it needs to be (a fair building)
71 *inmates* Florida's body is a metaphoric building in which she is hospitable to men, the 'inmates'.
74 *termers* the lawyers, students and litigants, men who came up to London in term time, when law courts were in session
75 *booted* i.e. prepared for riding. Since 'riding' could mean sexual intercourse, there is an innuendo.
76 s.d. [*retires*] This is the first of several moments in the play (see also l. 87) when a character remains on-stage but ceases to participate in the action.

AMORETTA
I'll call aloud, i'faith.
ALMACHILDES I'll stop your mouth.
AMORETTA
Upon my love to reputation 80
I'll tell the duchess once more.
ALMACHILDES 'Tis the way
To make her laugh a little.
AMORETTA She'll not think
That you dare use a maid of honour thus.
ALMACHILDES
Amsterdam swallow thee for a puritan
And Geneva cast thee up again, like she that sunk 85
At Charing Cross and rose again at Queenhithe!
AMORETTA
Ay, these are the holy fruits of the sweet vine sir.

[AMORETTA *withdraws*]

ALMACHILDES
Sweet venery be with thee and I at the tail of my wish! I am a little headstrong, and so are most of the company. I will to the witches; they say they have charms and 90 tricks to make a wench fall backwards and lead a man herself to a country house some mile out of the town, like a fire-drake. There be such whoreson kind girls and such bawdy witches, and I'll try conclusions.

Enter DUKE, DUCHESS, L[ORD] GOVERNOR, ANTONIO *and* ISABELLA, FRANCISCA

81–2 ed. ('Tis ... little *one line in* MS)
83 *maid of honour* unmarried, nobly born woman attending on a woman of the royal family
84 *Amsterdam* centre for puritans
85 *Geneva* centre for Calvinist puritans
85–6 In legend Elinor, queen of Edward I, denied (untruthfully) that she had murdered the Mayor of London's wife. She prayed that, if she lied, the earth might swallow her up and so she sank into the ground at Charing Cross and reappeared at Queenhithe.
87 *holy* ed. (holly MS) Amoretta is being ironic.
88–94 These lines may be verse in MS.
88 *venery* practice or pursuit of sexual pleasure, punning on 'vine', l. 87
tail The Latin for 'tail' is 'penis'.
89 *headstrong* with drink
91 *fall backwards* for sex
92 *country house* London citizens often went on day trips for sex to local country taverns.
93 *fire-drake* will-o'-the-wisp 94 *try conclusions* experiment

DUKE
A banquet yet? Why surely, my lord governor, 95
Bacchus could never boast of a day till now
To spread his power and make his glory known.

DUCHESS
Sir you've done nobly. Though in modesty
You keep it from us, know we understand so much –
All this day's cost 'tis your great love bestows 100
In honour of the bride, your virtuous niece.

GOVERNOR
In love to goodness and your presence madam –
So understood, 'tis rightly.

DUKE Now will I
Have a strange health after all these.

GOVERNOR What's that my
lord?

DUKE
A health in a strange cup – and't shall go round. 105

GOVERNOR
Your grace need not doubt that, sir, having seen
So many pledged already. This fair company
Cannot shrink now for one, so it end there.

DUKE
It shall, for all ends here; here's a full period.

[*Produces a cup made out of a human skull*]

GOVERNOR
A skull my lord?

DUKE Call it a soldier's cup, man. 110
Fie, how you fright the women! I have sworn
It shall go round, excepting only you, sir,
For your late sickness, and the bride herself,
Whose health it is.

ISABELLA [*Aside*] Marry, I thank heaven for that.

95 *yet* still to come

96 *Bacchus* god of wine

100–3 The duchess interprets the feasting as a compliment to Isabella, but the lord governor insists it is also a compliment to the duchess.

104 *health* toast

108 *Cannot . . . there* will not refuse one more drink so long as it is the last one

109 *period* ending of the drinking but also the end of life, which the skull represents

111 *Fie* The duke is addressing the cup.

112 *you* the lord governor

DUKE
Our duchess, I know, will pledge us, though the cup 115
Was once her father's head – which as a trophy
We'll keep till death in memory of that conquest.
He was the greatest foe our steel e'er struck at,
And he was bravely slain. Then took we thee
Into our bosom's love; thou madest the peace 120
For all thy country, thou, that beauty, did.
We're dearer than a father are we not?

DUCHESS
Yes, sir, by much.

DUKE And we shall find that straight.

ANTONIO
[*Aside*] That's an ill bride-cup for a marriage day;
I do not like the fate on't.

GOVERNOR Good my lord, 125
The duchess looks pale. Let her not pledge you there.

DUKE
Pale?

DUCHESS Sir not I.

DUKE See how your lordship fails now.
The rose's not fresher, nor the sun at rising
More comfortably pleasing.

DUCHESS [*To* ANTONIO] Sir to you,
The lord of this day's honour. [*Drinks*]

ANTONIO All first moving 130
From your grace, madam, and the duke's great
favour. [*Drinks*]
[*To* FRANCISCA] Sister it must.

FRANCISCA [*Aside*] This's the worst fright
that could come
To a concealed great belly. I'm with child,
And this will bring it out or make me come
Some seven weeks sooner than we maidens reckon. 135
[*Drinks*]

118 *steel* sword 119 *thee* the duchess
123 *straight* straight away
125 *fate* ed. (ffate MS)
the fate on't its ominous nature
126 *pledge* toast with drink 127 *fails* is wrong
128 *rose's* ed. (Rose' MS) 130 *moving* originating
132 *it must* you have (to drink)
This's ed. (this' MS)
133 *great belly* pregnant woman 134 *come* go into labour

DUCHESS
[*Aside*] Did ever cruel, barbarous act match this?
Twice hath his surfeits brought my father's memory
Thus spitefully and scornfully to mine eyes,
And I'll endure't no more. 'Tis in my heart since;
I'll be revenged as far as death can lead me. 140

ALMACHILDES
Am I the last man then? I may deserve
To be first one day. [*Drinks*]

GOVERNOR Sir it has gone round now.

DUKE
The round? An excellent way to train up soldiers.
Where's bride and bridegroom?

ANTONIO At your happy service.

DUKE
A boy tonight at least! I charge you look to't 145
Or I'll renounce you for industrious subjects.

ANTONIO
Your grace speaks like a worthy and tried soldier.
Exeunt [*all except* GASPERO]

GASPERO
And you'll do well, for one that ne'er tossed pike sir.
Exit

[Act I,] Scene ii

Enter HECATE

HECATE
Titty and Tiffin,
Suckin and Pidgen,
Liard and Robin,

139 *since* ever since

143 *round* the walk or circuit performed by the watch of a garrison as well as a drinking 'round'

145 *A boy tonight* i.e. conceive a boy. Superstition and medical science supposed that it required more vital spirits and heat to beget a boy than a girl; hence the pun at l. 146 on 'industrious'.

147 *tried soldier* with a pun based on the parallel of military and amorous combat, meaning a man whose sexual prowess is proven

148 *tossed pike* brandished arms, i.e. served as a soldier (also sexual innuendo)

0 s.d. ed. ('enter Heccat: & other witches: (with Properties, and Habbitts fitting.) MS) The 'other witches' who are tending the cauldron have to be off-stage for Almachildes to be reported (ll. 183–8) as nearly tripping into it and for Hecate to send Stadlin 'in' to 'feed' the vessel (ll. 36–7). Hecate must have the 'dead baby' with her at the beginning of the scene.

White spirits, black spirits,
Grey spirits, red spirits, 5
Devil-toad, devil-ram,
Devil-cat and devil dam.
Why Hoppo and Stadlin, Hellwain and Puckle!

STADLIN
[*Within*] Here, sweating at the vessel.

HECATE
Boil it well.

HOPPO [*Within*] It gallops now.

HECATE
Are the flames blue
enough? 10
Or shall I use a little seeton more?

STADLIN
[*Within*] The nips of fairies upon maids' white hips
Are not more perfect azure.

HECATE
Tend it carefully.
Send Stadlin to me with a brazen dish,
That I may fall to work upon these serpents, 15
And squeeze 'em ready for the second hour.
Why when?

[*Enter* STADLIN *with the dish*]

STADLIN Here's Stadlin and the dish.

HECATE
There, take this unbaptised brat;
[*Gives* STADLIN *a dead baby*]

1–7 Ed. (Titty ... Suckin / and ... Robin / white ... Speritts: / Deuill-Toad ... Dam. / MS)
1–7 *Titty ... devil dam* taken from Scot's *Discourse upon Devils and Spirits* appended to *Discovery of Witchcraft*, ch. 33, p. 455. Cf. V.ii.60–4.
3 *Liard* balsam poplar
7 *dam* mother. Cf. Tilley D 225, 'The Devil and his dam'.
8 *Hellwain* ed. (Hellwin MS)
Puckle ed. (Prickle MS)
10 *gallops* boils
blue This suggests unnatural happenings.
11 *seeton* not in *OED*; presumably a substance which produces blue flames. Dyce suggests 'seething'.
12–13 Cf. *Merry Wives of Windsor* V.v.45–6. It was commonly believed that fairies pinched lazy maids.
18 *unbaptised* and so unprotected from the witches. See Scot 10.8, where the recipe for 'witches' transportations' includes: 'The fat of young children, and seethe it with water in a brazen vessel, reserving the thickest of that which remaineth boiled in the bottom.' Cf. also Scot 3.1: 'So as, if there be any children unbaptised, or not guarded with the sign of the cross, or orisons; then the witches may and do catch them from their mothers' sides in the night, or out of their cradles, or otherwise kill them with their ceremonies; and after burial steal them out of their

Boil it well, preserve the fat;
You know 'tis precious to transfer 20
Our 'nointed flesh into the air,
In moonlight nights, o'er steeple tops,
Mountains and pine trees, that like pricks or stops
Seem to our height – high towers and roofs of princes
Like wrinkles in the earth. Whole provinces 25
Appear to our sight then even leek
A russet mole upon some lady's cheek,
When hundred leagues in air we feast and sing,
Dance, kiss and coll, use everything.
What young man can we wish to pleasure us 30
But we enjoy him in an incubus?
Thou know'st it Stadlin?

STADLIN Usually that's done.

HECATE

Last night thou got'st the Mayor of Whelplie's son.
I knew him by his black cloak lined with yellow;
I think thou'st spoiled the youth; he's but seventeen; 35
I'll have him the next mounting. Away, in!
Go feed the vessel for the second hour.

STADLIN

Where be the magical herbs?

HECATE They're down his throat,

His mouth crammed full, his ears and nostrils stuffed.
I thrust in *eleoselinum* lately, 40

---

graves, and seethe them in a cauldron, until their flesh be made potable. Of the thickest whereof they make ointments, whereby they ride in the air'.

21 *'nointed* anointed 22 *o'er* ed. (or MS)

23 *pricks or stops* dots, punctuation marks

26 *leek* obsolete form of like, for rhyme

29 *coll* embrace. See Scot 10.8: 'By this means . . . in a moon light night they seem to be carried in the air, to feasting, singing, dancing, kissing, culling, and other acts of venery, with such youths as they love and desire most'.

31 *incubus* evil spirit or demon which takes a man's form to have sexual intercourse with women when they are asleep. Scot discusses various incubus manifestations in 4.5, 4.9, 4.10, 4.11, 4.12. A *succubus* takes a woman's form to have intercourse with a sleeping man and so would seem to be the more appropriate term here.

33 *Whelplie's* ed. (Wlelplies MS) an invented name suggesting the youthful, whelp-like character of Stadlin's victim?

36 *mounting* flight and sexual encounter 38 *his* the dead baby's

40–5 *I thrust in . . . oleum* Cf. Scot 10.8: 'They put hereunto eleoselinum, aconitum, frondes populeas, and soot. Another receipt [recipe] to the same purpose. R. sium, acarum vulgare, pentaphyllon, the blood of a flitter-mouse, solanum somniferum, & oleum'.
eleoselinum parsley

Aconitum, frondes populeus and soot –
You may see that, he looks so black i'th' mouth –
Then *sium, acharum vulgaro* too,
Pentaphyllon, the blood of a flitter-mouse,
Solanum somnificum et oleum. 45

STADLIN
Then there's all Hecate.

HECATE
Is the heart of wax
Stuck full of magic needles?

STADLIN
'Tis done Hecate.

HECATE
And is the farmer's picture and his wife's
Laid down to th'fire yet?

STADLIN
They're a-roasting both, too.

HECATE
Good.
[*Exit* STADLIN]

Then their marrows are a-melting subtly, 50
And three months' sickness sucks up life in 'em.
They denied me often flour, barm and milk,
Goose grease and tar, when I ne'er hurt their charmings,
Their brew-locks, nor their batches, nor forespoke

---

41 *Aconitum* deadly poisonous plant, monk's head and wolf's bane. See *Masque of Queens* (p. 299): 'the juice of it, is like that liquor which the devil gives witches to sprinkle abroad, and do hurt, in the opinion of all the magic masters'.
frondes populeus poplar leaves

42 *black* ed. (back MS)

43 *sium* glabrous herb, yellow watercress
acharum vulgaro common myrtle

44 *Pentaphyllon* ed. following Scot ('Dentaphillon' MS); cinquefoil, literally five-leaved
flitter-mouse bat

45 *Solanum somnificum* sleep-inducing, deadly nightshade
oleum oil

46–7 *heart . . . needles* Scot 12.16 describes 'A charm teaching how to hurt whom you list with images of wax etc.' and the use of 'a heart of wax, and pricking the same with pins and needles'.

52–3 Denying a witch charity was commonly supposed to result in being bewitched; cf. *Macbeth* I.iii.4–10.

52 *barm* froth on fermenting liquors, used to leaven bread and cause fermentation in liquors

53 *charmings* variant form of churnings, the quantity of butter produced from a churn

54 *brew-locks* not in *OED*; variant on 'brew-lead', a leaden vessel used in brewing?
batches of bread
forespoke bewitched

Any of their breedings. Now I'll be meet with 'em. 55
Seven of their young pigs I've bewitched already
Of the last litter, nine ducklings, thirteen goslings – and a hog
Fell lame last Sunday after evensong too –
And mark how their sheep prosper or what sop
Each milch-kine gives to th' pail. I'll send those snakes 60
Shall milk 'em all beforehand. The dewed-skirted dairy wenches
Shall stroke dry dugs for this and go home cursing.
I'll mar their syllabubs and frothy feastings
Under cows' bellies with the parish youths.
Where's Firestone? our son Firestone!

Enter FIRESTONE

FIRESTONE
Here am I mother. 65

HECATE
Take in this brazen dish full of dear ware.

[*Gives him dish*]

Thou shalt have all when I die – and that will be
Even just at twelve o'clock at night come three year.

FIRESTONE
And may you not have one o'clock into th' dozen, mother?

HECATE
No. 70

FIRESTONE
Your spirits are then more unconscionable than bakers; you'll have lived then, mother, six-score year to the hundred – and methinks after six-score years the devil might give you a cast – for he's a fruiterer too and has

55 *breedings* of animals on the farm
be meet with be even with
57 Lineation is as in MS. Other editors regularise the verse.
58 *after . . . too* Attending evensong might be thought to protect the farmer, and so Hecate is particularly proud of this exploit.
59 *sop* liquid (here milk) in which bread, etc. is dipped
60 *milch-kine* milk cows
62 *stroke . . . dugs* i.e. the cows will yield no milk
63 *syllabubs* drink or dish made from milk or cream curdled by a mixture of wine, cider, etc., often sweetened and flavoured
71 *unconscionable* without regard for conscience
74 *cast* chance. Firestone's joke is laboured. If the devil gives 120 years, i.e. a dozen × 10, he could round it up to a baker's dozen or 13.

been from the beginning; the first apple that e'er was 75
eaten came through his fingers. The costermonger's,
then, I hold to be the ancientest trade, though some
would have the tailor pricked down before him.

HECATE

Go, and take heed you shed not by the way.
The hour must have her portion, 'tis dear syrup; 80
Each charmed drop is able to confound
A family consisting of nineteen
Or one-and-twenty feeders.

FIRESTONE [*Aside*] Marry, here's stuff indeed!
Dear syrup call you it? A little thing
Would make me give you a dram on't in a posset, 85
And cut you three years shorter.

HECATE

Thou'rt now about some villainy?

FIRESTONE

Not I forsooth. [*Aside*] Truly the devil's in her, I think.
How one villain smells out another straight! There's no
knavery but is nosed like a dog and can smell out a dog's 90
meaning. [*To* HECATE] Mother I pray give me leave to
ramble abroad tonight with the Nightmare, for I have a
great mind to overlay a fat parson's daughter.

HECATE

And who shall lie with me then?

FIRESTONE

The great cat for one night mother. 'Tis but a night – 95
Make shift with him for once.

HECATE You're a kind son!
But 'tis the nature of you all, I see that.
You had rather hunt after strange women still
Than lie with your own mothers. Get thee gone.

75 *first apple* Eve's in the Garden of Eden
76 *costermonger* fruit seller
78 *pricked* written or noted down (with a pun on 'prick' meaning penis)
80 *hour . . . portion* spells or poisons must be matched to auspicious times
81 *confound* kill
85 *posset* drink of hot milk curdled with ale, wine, sugar and spices
89 *villain* MS could be read as 'villainy'.
straight straight away
90–1 *nosed . . . meaning* i.e. knavery has as good a nose for smelling as a dog and is particularly good at smelling out the meanings of other knaves
92 *Nightmare* Cf. Scot 4.11. 'The mare' is explained as a spirit 'oppressing many in their sleep so sore, as they are not able to call for help, or stir themselves under the burden of that heavy humour'.
95 *cat* presumably Malkin

Sweat thy six ounces out about the vessel 100
And thou shalt play at midnight. The Nightmare
Shall call thee when it walks.

FIRESTONE Thanks, most sweet
mother.

Exit

Enter SEBASTIAN

HECATE

Urchins, elves, hags, satyrs, pans, fauns, Silens, Kit-
with-the-candlestick, tritons, centaurs, dwarves, imps,
the Spoorn, the Mare, the Man i'th'oak, the Hellwain, 105
the Fire-drake, the Puckle. A ab hur hus!

SEBASTIAN

[*Aside*] Heaven knows with what unwillingness and hate
I enter this damned place – but such extremes
Of wrongs in love fight 'gainst religious knowledge,
That were I led by this disease to deaths 110
As numberless as creatures that must die,
I could not shun the way. I know what 'tis

102 s.d. *Enter* SEBASTIAN Most editors read this as an early entrance and relocate it to the end of Hecate's charm. However the MS positioning allows her performance to be played to impress her prospective client.

103–6 *Urchins . . . the Puckle* Cf. Scot 7.15: 'they have so fraid us with bull beggars, spirits, witches, urchins, elves, hags, fairies, satyrs, pans, fauns, Silens, Kit-with-the-candlestick, tritons, centaurs, dwarves, giants, imps, calcars, conjurors, nymphs, changelings, *incubus*, Robin Goodfellow, the Spoorn, the Mare, the Man in the oak, the Hellwain, the Fire-drake, the Puckle, Tom Thumb'.

103 *Urchins* goblins or elves, supposed to take the shape of a hedgehog
satyrs mythical creatures, half-human, half-beast, fabled for their roughness and their appetite
pans mythical creatures, above the waist like men, below like goats (the goat is proverbial for lust). Pan is the name of a Nature god.
fauns wood-gods
Silens ed. (Silence MS) Sileni, wood gods, satyrs

103–4 *Kit-with-the-candlestick* will-o'-the'-wisp

104 *tritons* sea monsters of semi-human form
centaurs monsters with the body and legs of a horse but a man's upper body and head

105 *Spoorn* This has not yet been certainly explained by scholars, but it is presumably some kind of spectre or phantom.
Mare nightmare
the Man i'th'oak so far unexplained, but presumably a spirit (with suggestions of Druid culture?)

106 *the Fire-drake* See I.i.93.

106 *A ab hur hus* Scot 12.14 quotes this as a charm 'Against the toothache'. This comic phrase suggests an exaggerated performance by Hecate.

To pity madmen now. They're wretched things
That ever were created, if they be
Of woman's making and her faithless vows. 115
I fear they're now a-kissing. What's o'clock?
'Tis now but supper-time, but night will come –
And all new-married couples make short suppers.
[*To* HECATE] Whate'er thou art, I have no spare time to
fear thee;
My horrors are so strong and great already, 120
That thou seem'st nothing. Up and laze not.
Hadst thou my business, thou couldst ne'er sit so;
'Twould firk thee into air a thousand mile
Beyond thy ointments. I would I were read
So much in thy black power as mine own griefs. 125
I'm in great need of help; wilt give me any?

HECATE
Thy boldness takes me bravely. We're all sworn
To sweat for such a spirit. See, I regard thee,
I rise and bid thee welcome. What's thy wish now?

SEBASTIAN
Oh my heart swells with't. I must take breath first. 130

HECATE
Is't to confound some enemy on the seas?
It may be done tonight. Stadlin's within;
She raises all your sudden, ruinous storms
That shipwreck barks and tears up growing oaks,
Flies over houses and takes *Anno Domini* 135
Out of a rich man's chimney – a sweet place for't!
He would be hanged ere he would set his own years
there;
They must be chambered in a five-pound picture,
A green silk curtain drawn before the eyes on't,

123 *firk* jerk, beat, whip
124 *ointments* for flying as in ll. 19–21
125 *as* ed. (and MS)
127 *takes* pleases
bravely a great deal
sworn in compact with the devil
134 *barks* boats
135 *Anno Domini* the year that the house was built, marked on a stone tablet and placed in the chimney
136 *sweet* meant ironically, as a chimney smells of soot
137 *years* his age
138–9 *chambered . . . on't* They must be recorded in a portrait costing five pounds (which noted the sitter's age) with a green silk curtain drawn over it.

His rotten diseased years. Or dost thou envy 140
The fat prosperity of any neighbour?
I'll call forth Hoppo and her incantation
Can straight destroy the young of all his cattle,
Blast vineyards, orchards, meadows or in one night
Transport his dung, hay, corn, by ricks, whole stacks, 145
Into thine own ground.

SEBASTIAN This would come most richly
now
To many a country grazier – but my envy
Lies not so low as cattle, corn, or vines;
'Twill trouble your best powers to give me ease.

HECATE
Is it to starve up generation? 150
To strike a barrenness in man or woman?

SEBASTIAN Hah!

HECATE
Hah? Did you feel me there? I knew your grief.

SEBASTIAN
Can there be such things done?

HECATE Are these the skins
Of serpents? these of snakes?

SEBASTIAN I see they are.

[HECATE *gives them to* SEBASTIAN]

HECATE
So sure into what house these are conveyed, 155
Knit with these charmed and retentive knots,
Neither the man begets nor woman breeds;
No, nor performs the least desires of wedlock,
Being then a mutual duty. I could give thee
Chiroconita, adincantida 160
Archimadon, marmaritin, calicia,

143–5 *destroy . . . stacks* Cf. Scot 12.5: witches can 'when they list invisibly transfer the third part of their neighbours' dung, hay, corn, &c: into their own ground'.

150 *starve . . . generation* The reference to inability to generate children may be an allusion to the Essex divorce. Scot 4.4 contains several comical reports of such bewitchings. Scot 4.8 looks at cures and comments that if 'the witchcraft be perpetual . . . the wife may have a divorce of course'.

152 *I knew . . . grief* typical charlatan's trick, claiming prescience after several wrong guesses

157–9 Cf. Scot 12.6: 'men cannot beget, nor women bring forth any children, nor yet accomplish the duty of wedlock'.

160–1 *Chiroconita . . . calicia* all poisons. Scot 6.3, listing 'magical herbs and stones', includes: '*marmaritin*, whereby spirits might be raised: *archimedon*, which would make one bewray in his sleep, all the secrets in his heart: *adincantida, calicia, mevais, chirocineta* &c: which had all their several virtues, or rather poisons'.

Which I could sort to villainous barren ends –
But this leads the same way. More I could instance:
As the same needles thrust into their pillows
That sows and socks up dead men in their sheets: 165
A privy gristle of a man that hangs
After sunset – good, excellent! Yet all's there sir.

SEBASTIAN
You could not do a man that special kindness
To part 'em utterly now? Could you do that?

HECATE
No, time must do't. We cannot disjoin wedlock; 170
'Tis of heaven's fastening. Well may we raise jars,
Jealousies, strifes and heart-burning disagreements,
Like a thick scurf o'er life, as did our master
Upon that patient miracle – but the work itself
Our power cannot disjoint.

SEBASTIAN I depart happy 175
In what I have then, being constrained to this –
[*Aside*] And grant, you greater powers that dispose
men,
That I may never need this hag again! *Exit*

HECATE
I know he loves me not, nor there's no hope on't;
'Tis for the love of mischief I do this – 180
And that we're sworn to, the first oath we take.

[*Enter* FIRESTONE]

FIRESTONE
Oh mother, mother!

HECATE What's the news with thee now?

FIRESTONE
There's the bravest young gentleman within, and the fineliest drunk; I thought he would have fallen into the

162 *sort* arrange

164–5 *needles . . . sheets* Cf. Scot 6.7: love charms include 'needles wherewith dead bodies are sown or socked into their sheets (shrouds)'.

166 *privy gristle* i.e. penis

170–1 Cf. *Macbeth* I.iii.24–5. Witches' powers were supposed to be weaker than Christianity, faith in which protected people.

171 *jars* discords

173 *our master* the devil

174 *that patient miracle* Job, whose suffering was a test of faith and of love of God *the work* the marriage

181 Cf. ll. 127–8.

183 *bravest* most expensively dressed, most splendid

vessel. He stumbled at a pipkin of child's grease, reeled 185
against Stadlin, overthrew her and, in the tumbling-cast,
struck up old Puckle's heels with her clothes over her
ears.

HECATE
Hoyday!

FIRESTONE
I was fain to throw the cat upon her to save her honesty, 190
and all little enough. I cried out still 'I pray be covered!'
See where he comes now mother.

Enter ALMACHILDES

ALMACHILDES
Call you these witches?
They be tumblers, methinks, very flat tumblers.

HECATE
'Tis Almachildes – fresh blood stirs in me – 195
The man that I have lusted to enjoy.
I have had him thrice in incubus already.

ALMACHILDES
Is your name Goody Hag?

HECATE
'Tis anything.
Call me the horrid'st and unhallowed'st things
That life and nature trembles at – for thee 200
I'll be the same. Thou com'st for a love-charm now?

ALMACHILDES
Why thou'rt a witch I think.

HECATE
Thou shalt have choice of twenty, wet or dry.

ALMACHILDES
Nay, let's have dry ones.

185 *pipkin* a small earthenware pot used chiefly in cookery

186 *tumbling-cast* somersault

187–8 *clothes ... ears* Women did not wear underclothes. Firestone's 'I pray be covered!' (l. 191), referring normally to the putting on of a hat, here refers to covering up Puckle's pubic hair.

189 *Hoyday* form of heyday, an exclamation of surprise

190–1 *to ... enough* to save her from disgrace even though there was little reputation left to save and/or the cat was not big enough to cover her private parts

194 *flat* prostrate on the ground but also absolute, downright tumblers

197 *incubus* actually *succubus*. See note to l. 31 above.

198 *Goody* short for 'goodwife', a civil term usually applied to a married woman of the poorest class

202 a proverbial response to a good guess about another's intentions (see Tilley W 585)

HECATE
If thou wilt use't by way of cup and potion, 205
I'll give thee a remora shall bewitch her straight.

ALMACHILDES
A remora? what's that?

HECATE
A little suck-stone;
Some call it a sea-lamprey, a small fish.

ALMACHILDES
And must't be buttered?

HECATE
The bones of a green frog too, wondrous precious,
The flesh consumed by pismires.

ALMACHILDES
Pismires? Give me a chamberpot! 210

FIRESTONE
[*Aside*] You shall see him go nigh to be so unmannerly,
He'll make water before my mother anon.

ALMACHILDES
And now you talk of frogs, I have somewhat here;
I come not empty pocketed from a banquet;
I learned that of my haberdasher's wife. 215
Look Goody Witch, there's a toad in marchpane for you.

[*Gives it* HECATE]

HECATE
Oh sir, you've fitted me.

ALMACHILDES
And here's a spawn or two
Of the same paddock-brood too for your son.

[*Gives it* FIRESTONE]

206–10 Cf. Scot 6.7: 'The toys, which are said to procure love, and are exhibited in their poison loving cups, are these: the hair growing in the nethermost part of a wolf's tail, a wolf's yard, a little fish called *remora*, the brain of a cat, of a newt, or of a lizard: the bone of a green frog, the flesh thereof being consumed with pismires or ants; the left bone whereof engendereth (as they say) love; the bone on the right side, hate'.

206 *remora* eel-like, sucking fish, believed to be able to halt a ship by sucking at it

207 *suck-stone* as Hecate says, another name for the remora

208 *sea-lamprey* ed. (Stalamprey MS)
must't be ed. (must'be MS)

210 *Pismires* ants

214 Cf. *Women Beware Women* III.i.267–8.

216 *marchpane* marzipan

217 *fitted* suited, pleased

218 *paddock-brood* brood of toads

FIRESTONE
I thank your worship sir. How comes your handkercher
so sweetly thus berayed? Sure 'tis wet sucket sir. 220

ALMACHILDES
'Tis nothing but the syrup the toad spit.
Take all I prithee.

HECATE
This was kindly done sir,
And you shall sup with me tonight for this.

ALMACHILDES
How? Sup with thee? Dost think I'll eat fried rats
And pickled spiders?

HECATE
No; I can command, sir, 225
The best meat i'th' whole province for my friends,
And reverently served in too.

ALMACHILDES
How?

HECATE
In good fashion.

ALMACHILDES
Let me but see that, and I'll sup with you.

She conjures and enter [MALKIN, *a spirit like*] *a cat, playing on a fiddle, and spirits with meat*

The cat and fiddle? An excellent ordinary!
You had a devil once in a fox-skin? 230

HECATE
Oh I have him still. Come walk with me sir.

Exeunt [*all but* FIRESTONE]

FIRESTONE
How apt and ready is a drunkard now to reel to the devil! Well I'll even in and see how he eats – and I'll be hanged if I be not the fatter of the twain with laughing at him. *Exit* 235

219 *handkercher* handkerchief

220 *berayed* dirtied, stained
sucket See I.i.67.

228 s.d. *She conjures* This offers the best possibilities for spectacle, as suggested by the opening MS s.d. (see note to 0.s.d. above).

229 *ordinary* the kind of tavern providing fixed-price meals. 'The Cat and Fiddle' is still a pub name today.

234 *fatter* 'Laugh and be fat' is a proverbial expression; see R. W. Dent, *Proverbial Language in English Drama Exclusive of Shakespeare 1495–1616* (1984), L 91.

Act II, Scene i

Enter ANTONIO *and* GASPERO

GASPERO
Good sir, whence springs this sadness? Trust me, sir,
You look not like a man was married yesterday.
There could come no ill tidings since last night
To cause that discontent. I was wont to know all
Before you had a wife sir. You ne'er found me 5
Without those parts of manhood: trust and secrecy.

ANTONIO
I will not tell thee this.

GASPERO Not your true servant sir?

ANTONIO
True? You'll all flout according to your talent,
The best a man can keep of you – and a hell 'tis
For masters to pay wages to be laughed at. 10
Give order that two cocks be boiled to jelly.

GASPERO
How? two cocks boiled to jelly?

ANTONIO
Fetch half an ounce of pearl. *Exit*

GASPERO This is a cullis
For a consumption – and I hope one night
Has not brought you to need the cook already, 15
And some part of the goldsmith. What, two trades
In four and twenty hours and less time?
Pray heaven the surgeon and the pothecary
Keep out and then 'tis well. You'd better fortune,
As far as I see, with your strumpet sojourner, 20
Your little four nobles a week. I ne'er knew you

8 *flout* scoff at, mock

13 *pearl* Antonio hopes to cure his impotence by eating rich broth containing dissolved pearl. Gold was also used in such concoctions (see l. 16).
cullis broth

16–17 *What . . . time?* Gaspero is shocked that Antonio needs two trades – goldsmiths and cooks – to fortify him so soon after his marriage.

18 *surgeon . . . pothecary* If Antonio needs these additional trades, he'll be on his last legs.

20 *strumpet sojourner* i.e. Florida, his kept mistress, 'sojourner' suggesting the temporariness of the arrangement

21 *nobles* coins worth 6 shillings and 8 pence (about 33p.). For a perspective on Florida's going rates see *A Mad World My Masters* III.iii.150–1, where Follywit scorns the 'two-shilling brothel, / Twelvepenny panderism'.

Eat one panada all the time you've kept her –
And is't in one night now come up to two-cock broth?
I wonder at the alteration strangely.

Enter FRANCISCA

FRANCISCA
Good morrow Gasper.
GASPERO Your hearty wishes, mistress, 25
And your sweet dreams come upon you.
FRANCISCA What's that
sir?
GASPERO
In a good husband; that's my real meaning.
FRANCISCA
Saw you my brother lately?
GASPERO Yes.
FRANCISCA I met him now
As sad, methought, as grief could make a man.
Know you the cause?
GASPERO Not I. I know nothing 30
But half an ounce of pearl and kitchen business,
Which I will see performed with all fidelity.
I'll break my trust in nothing, not in porridge, I. *Exit*
FRANCISCA
I have the hardest fortune, I think, of a hundred
gentlewomen. 35
Some can make merry with a friend seven year
And nothing seen – as perfect a maid still,
To the world's knowledge, as she came from rocking.
But 'twas my luck, at the first hour, forsooth,
To prove too fruitful. Sure I'm near my time. 40
I'm yet but a young scholar, I may fail
In my account – but certainly I do not.
These bastards come upon poor venturing gentlewomen ten to one faster than your legitimate children. If I had been married, I'll be hanged if I had been with child so 45 soon now. When they are once husbands, they'll be

22 *panada* rich bread pudding
34–6 ed. (I . . . a-hundred / Gentlewomen; . . . yeere, MS)
36 *friend* lover
38 *rocking* in the cradle
42 Francisca rechecks her calculations here.
43–52 prose ed. (*verse in* MS)
43 *venturing* gambling or investing sexually (as in the term 'merchant adventurers')
46 *once* This could be 'oure' in MS.

whipped ere they take such pains as a friend will do: to come by water to the backdoor at midnight: there stay perhaps an hour in all weathers with a pair of reeking watermen laden with bottles of wine, chewets and currant custards. I may curse those egg-pies – they are meat that help forward too fast. 50

This hath been usual with me night by night –
Honesty forgive me – when my brother has been
Dreaming of no such junkets; yet he hath fared 55
The better for my sake, though he little think
For what – nor must he ever. My friend promised me
To provide safely for me and devise
A means to save my credit here i'th'house.
My brother sure would kill me if he knew't, 60
And powder up my friend and all his kindred
For an East Indian voyage.

Enter ISABELLA

ISABELLA
Alone sister?

FRANCISCA
[*Aside*] No, there's another with me, though you see't not.
[*To* ISABELLA] Morrow, sweet sister. How have you slept tonight?

ISABELLA
More than I thought I should; I've had good rest. 65

FRANCISCA
I'm glad to hear't.

ISABELLA
Sister methinks you are too long alone,
And lose much good time, sociable and honest.
I'm for the married life; I must praise that now.

48 *come by water . . . backdoor* Riverside Thames houses could be entered thus unobserved from the street.

50 *chewets* minced meat or fish pies

51 *currant* ed. (Curran MS)
egg-pies Eggs were regarded as aphrodisiacs.

55 *junkets* feastings, merrymakings

55–6 *fared / The better* i.e. he has had better 'fare' – the food and gifts Aberzanes brought – and he has benefited since Aberzanes' and Francisca's discretion has kept his family reputation intact

61–2 *powder . . . voyage* i.e. Antonio would have Almachildes and his family sent as far away as possible from Francisca

61 *powder up* preserve meat by salting

65 i.e. she's had no sex because of Sebastian's charm

FRANCISCA

I cannot blame you, sister, to commend it.
You have happened well, no doubt, on a kind husband, 70
And that's not every woman's fortune, sister.
You know if he were any but my brother,
My praises should not leave him yet so soon.

ISABELLA

I must acknowledge, sister, that my life
Is happily blessed with him. He is no gamester, 75
That ever I could find or hear of yet,
Nor midnight surfeiter. He does intend
To leave tobacco too.

FRANCISCA Why here's a husband!

ISABELLA

He saw it did offend me and swore freely
He'd ne'er take pleasure in a toy again 80
That should displease me. Some knights' wives in town
Will have great hope, upon his reformation,
To bring their husbands' breaths into th'old fashion,
And make 'em kiss like Christians, not like pagans.

FRANCISCA

I promise you, sister, 'twill be a worthy work 85
To put down all these pipers; 'tis great pity
There should not be a statute against them,
As against fiddlers.

ISABELLA These good offices,
If you'd a husband, you might exercise
To th' good o'th' commonwealth, and do much profit. 90
Beside, it is a comfort to a woman
T'have children, sister, a great blessing certainly.

75 *gamester* gambler for money and sexual pleasure. See the play by James Shirley entitled *The Gamester*.

80 *toy* trifle

81 *knights' ... town* The wives of knights came to London with their husbands; the beginnings of the 'Season', the social focus on London, has been traced to this period. Knights and gentry would come up to London from the shires to transact business and litigation during the legal Term-times. There was also an increase in the number of knights in the reign of James I because the king sold knighthoods to wealthy citizens.

84 *pagans* Tobacco smoking was customary among Native Americans and colonisers. King James published a polemic against smoking entitled *A Counterblast to Tobacco*.

86 *pipers* pipe-smokers

87–8 *statute ... fiddlers* Chambers, vol. 4, pp. 324, 337, records statutes against wandering minstrels in 1598 and 1604.

FRANCISCA
They will come fast enough.
ISABELLA Not so fast neither
As they're still welcome to an honest woman.
FRANCISCA
[*Aside*] How near she comes to me! I protest she grates 95
My very skin.
ISABELLA Were I conceived with child,
Beshrew my heart, I should be so proud on't.
FRANCISCA
That's natural; pride is a kind of swelling.
[*Aside*] And yet I've small cause to be proud of mine.
ISABELLA
You are no good companion for a wife; 100
Get you a husband, prithee, sister, do,
That I may ask your counsel now and then.
'Twill mend your discourse much; you maids know nothing.
FRANCISCA
No, we are fools – [*Aside*] but commonly we prove
Quicker mothers than you that have husbands. 105
I'm sure I shall else. I may speak for one.

Enter ANTONIO

ANTONIO
[*Aside*] I will not look upon her; I'll pass by,
And make as though I see her not.
ISABELLA Why sir,
Pray your opinion, by the way, with leave sir;
I'm counselling your sister here to marry. 110
ANTONIO
To marry? Soft, the priest is not at leisure yet –
Some five year hence. Would you fain marry sister?
FRANCISCA
I have no such hunger to't sir. [*Aside*] For I think
I've a good bit that well may stay my stomach,
As well as any that broke fast a sinner. 115
ANTONIO
Though she seem tall of growth, she's short in years

105 *Quicker* a pun on the speed of conception and the live (quick) baby in the womb
mothers i.e. subject to 'the mother', hysteria
106 *else* if it is not believed
108–9 Isabella has to bid for Antonio's attention repeatedly.
114 *good bit* her pregnancy, which reins in her desire for marriage

Of some that seem much lower. How old sister?
Not seventeen, for a yard of lawn!

FRANCISCA
Not yet sir.

ANTONIO I told you so.

FRANCISCA
[*Aside*] I would he'd laid a wager of old shirts rather; 120
I shall have more need of them shortly – and yet
A yard of lawn will serve for a christening-cloth;
I have use for everything as my case stands.

ISABELLA
I care not if I try my voice this morning,
But I have got a cold, sir, by your means. 125

ANTONIO
I'll strive to mend that fault.

ISABELLA I thank you sir.

Song

In a maiden-time professed,
Then we say that life is best.
Tasting once the married life,
Then we only praise the wife. 130
There's but one state more to try,
Which makes women laugh or cry –
Widow, widow. Of these three,
The middle's best and that give me.

ANTONIO
There's thy reward. [*Kisses her*]

ISABELLA I will not grumble, sir, 135
Like some musician; if more come, 'tis welcome.

FRANCISCA
[*Aside*] Such tricks has made me do all that I've done;
Your kissing married folks spoils all the maids
That ever live i'th' house with 'em.

Enter ABERZANES [*and* SERVANTS *with bags and bottles*]

Oh here
He comes with his bags and bottles; he was born 140
To lead poor water-men and I.

118 *for* I'll bet for
120 *shirts* Francisca is going to need old cloths for childbirth.
127 See Appendix (p. 89) for the music and two further verses of this song.
138 *spoils* corrupts
139 s.d. *bags* with food, the 'bakemeats' inside
139–40 ed. (that . . . comes / with . . . borne MS)

ABERZANES
Go, fellows, into th' larder; let the bakemeats
Be sorted by themselves.

ANTONIO Why sir –

ABERZANES
Look the canary bottles be well stopped;
The three of claret shall be drunk at dinner. 145
[*Exeunt* SERVANTS]

ANTONIO
My good sir, you're too plenteous of these courtesies,
Indeed you are; forbear 'em, I beseech ye.
I know no merit in me but poor love
And a true friend's well-wishing that can cause
This kindness in excess. [*Aside*] I'th' state that I am, 150
I shall go near to kick this fellow shortly
And send him downstairs with his bag and baggage.
Why comes he now I'm married? There's the point.
[*To* ABERZANES] I pray forbear these things.

ABERZANES Alas, you
know, sir,
These idle toys which you call courtesies, 155
They cost me nothing but my servants' travail.
One office must be kind, sir, to another;
You know the fashion. What, the gentlewoman
Your sister's sad methinks.

ANTONIO I know no cause she has.

FRANCISCA
[*Aside*] Nor shall you, by my good will. [*Aside* to
ABERZANES] What do you mean sir? 160
Shall I stay here to shame myself and you?
The time may be tonight for aught you know.

ABERZANES
[*To her*] Peace! There's means wrought I tell thee.

FRANCISCA [*To him*] Ay
sir, when?

Enter SEBASTIAN [*disguised as* CELIO] *and* GENTLEMAN

ANTONIO
How now? What's he?

ISABELLA Oh this is the man, sir,

144 *canary* light, sweet wine from the Canary isles
156 *travail* labour
157 *office* court official
163 s.d. From now on until the final scene Sebastian appears in disguise as Celio.

I entertained this morning for my service; 165
Please you to give your liking.

ANTONIO Yes, he's welcome;
I like him not amiss. [*To* SEBASTIAN] Thou wouldst speak business,
Wouldst thou not?

SEBASTIAN Yes; may it please you, sir,
There is a gentleman from the northern parts
Hath brought a letter, as it seems, in haste. 170

ANTONIO
From whom?

GENTLEMAN Your bonny lady mother, sir.

[*Gives letter to* ANTONIO]

ANTONIO
You're kindly welcome sir. How doth she?

GENTLEMAN
I left her heal varray well sir.

[ANTONIO *reads the*] *letter*

I pray send your sister down with all speed to me; I hope it will prove much for her good in the way of her 175 preferment. Fail me not, I desire you, son, nor let any excuse of hers withhold her. I have sent, ready furnished, horse and man for her.

ABERZANES
[*Aside to* FRANCISCA] Now, have I thought upon you?

FRANCISCA [*To him*] Peace, good sir.
You're worthy of a kindness another time. 180

ANTONIO
Her will shall be obeyed. Sister prepare yourself.
You must down with all speed.

FRANCISCA [*Aside*] I know down I must –
And good speed send me!

ANTONIO 'Tis our mother's pleasure.

165 *entertained* received into employ

166 *liking* approval

169 *northern parts* Scotland, to judge from the accent. Parodies of Scottish accents, reflecting on James I and his Scottish favourites (including Robert Carr), got several playwrights (e.g. Jonson, Chapman and Marston, the authors of *Eastward Ho!*, and John Day, author of *The Isle of Gulls*) into serious trouble. The joke is more obtrusive here given that the notional setting is Ravenna.

173 *heal varray well* 'health very well' in phonetically spelt joke Scottish

176 *preferment* advancement

182 *down I must* I must undergo childbirth

183 *speed* success

FRANCISCA
Good sir, write back again and certify her
I'm at my heart's wish here. I'm with my friends, 185
And can be but well, say.

ANTONIO You shall pardon me sister;
I hold it no wise part to contradict her,
Nor would I counsel you to't.

FRANCISCA 'Tis so uncouth
Living i'th' country now I'm used to'th' city,
That I shall ne'er endure't.

ABERZANES Perhaps, forsooth, 190
'Tis not her meaning you shall live there long.
I do not think but after a month or so
You'll be sent up again; that's my conceit.
However, let her have her will.

ANTONIO Ay, good sir,
Great reason 'tis she should.

ISABELLA I am sorry, sister, 195
'Tis our hard fortune thus to part so soon.

FRANCISCA
The sorrow will be mine.

ANTONIO Please you walk in sir.
We'll have one health into those northern parts –
[*Aside*] Though I be sick at heart.

ABERZANES Ay, sir, a deep one –

Exeunt [ISABELLA, ANTONIO *and* GENTLEMAN]

[*Aside to* FRANCISCA] Which you shall pledge too.

FRANCISCA [*To* ABERZANES] You
shall pardon me; 200
I have pledged one too deep already sir.

ABERZANES
[*To* FRANCISCA] Peace; all's provided for. Thy wine's
laid in,
Sugar and spice, the place not ten mile hence.
What cause have maids now to complain of men,
When a farmhouse can make all whole again? 205

Exeunt [FRANCISCA *and* ABERZANES]

SEBASTIAN
It takes! He's no content. How well she bears it yet.
Hardly myself can find so much from her

193 *conceit* opinion
198 *have . . . health* drink a health
201 a reference to her pregnancy
206 *It takes!* the spell is working

That am acquainted with the cold disease.
Oh honesty's a rare wealth in a woman!
It knows no want, at least will express none, 210
Not in a look. Yet I'm not throughly happy.
His ill does me no good. Well may it keep me
From open rage and madness for a time,
But I feel heart's grief in the same place still.
What makes the greatest torment 'mongst lost souls? 215
'Tis not so much the horror of their pains,
Though they be infinite, as the loss of joys;
It is that deprivation is the mother
Of all the groans in hell, and here on earth
Of all the red sighs in the hearts of lovers. 220
Still she's not mine, that can be no man's else
Till I be nothing, if religion
Have the same strength for me as't has for others.
Holy vows witness that our souls were married!

Enter GASPERO *and* L[ORD] GOVERNOR [*with* GENTLEMEN]

GASPERO
[*To* SEBASTIAN] Where are you sir? Come, pray give your attendance; 225
Here's my lord governor come.

GOVERNOR
Where's our new kindred?
Not stirring yet, I think?

GASPERO
Yes, my good lord.
Please you walk near?

GOVERNOR
Come, gentlemen, we'll enter.
[*Exeunt all except* SEBASTIAN]

SEBASTIAN
I've done't upon a breach; this's a less venture. [*Exit*]

208 *cold disease* lack of sexual fulfilment
211 *throughly* thoroughly
220 *red sighs* lovelorn sighs
229 i.e. I have successfully assalted a fortress in war; Isabella will be easier to overcome than that was
this's ed. (this' MS)

[Act II,] Scene ii

Enter ALMACHILDES

ALMACHILDES

What a mad toy took me to sup with witches?
Fie of all drunken humours! By this hand,
I could beat myself when I think on't – and the rascals
Made me good cheer too, and to my understanding
then
Ate some of every dish and spoiled the rest. 5
But coming to my lodging I remember
I was as hungry as a tired foot-post.

[*Takes a ribbon from his pocket*]

What's this? Oh 'tis the charm her hagship gave me
For my duchess' obstinate woman, wound about
A threepenny silk ribbon of three colours: 10
[*Reads*] *Necte tribus nodis ternos, Amoretta, colores.*
Amoretta – why there's her name indeed –
Necte, Amoretta – again, two bouts –
Nodo et 'Veneris' dic 'vincula necte' –
Nay, if *Veneris* be one, I'm sure there's no dead flesh
in't. 15
If I should undertake to construe this now,
I should make a fine piece of work of it;
For few young gallants are given to good construction
Of anything – hardly of their best friends' wives,

1 *toy* foolish, fantastic notion
4 *to . . . then* from what I (in my drunken state) could make sense of
5 *Ate* ed. (Eat MS)
spoiled messed up
7 *hungry* Scot 3.2 reports that after witches' banquets 'at their return home they are like to starve for hunger'.
foot-post foot courier
8–15 For this section see Introduction, p. xiii.
11 *Necte . . . colores* Virgil, *Eclogues* 8.77–8. Middleton substitutes 'Amoretta' for 'Amaryllis'. The Loeb Virgil gives the translation 'Weave, Amaryllis, three hues in three knots; weave them, Amaryllis, I beg, and say, "Chains of love I weave" '. Mistranslation jokes were generally popular in plays; for an example in Middleton's work see *CM* I.i.65–77.
13 *bouts* knots or twists
14 *Nodo* Virgil has 'modo', but the 'mistake' is needed for the joke on 'noddy'.
necte Virgil has 'necto'.
15 *dead flesh* bawdy, i.e. the flesh will rise to the occasion
16 *construe* explain, translate

Sisters or nieces. Let me see what I can do now. 20
Necte tribus nodis – Nick of the tribe of noddies –
Ternos colores – that makes turned colours –
Nodo et Veneris – goes to his venery like a noddy –
Dic Vincula – with Dick the vintner's boy.
Here were a sweet charm now if this were the meaning 25
on't, and very likely to overcome an honourable gentlewoman. The whoreson old hellcat would have given me
the brain of a cat once in my handkercher – I bad her
make sauce with't, with a vengeance! – and a little bone
in the nethermost part of a wolf's tail – I bad her pick 30
her teeth with't, with a pestilence! Nay, this is somewhat
cleanly yet and handsome; a coloured ribbon – a fine,
gentle charm – a man may give't his sister, his brother's
wife, ordinarily.

Enter AMORETTA

See, here she comes, luckily. 35

AMORETTA
Blessed powers, what secret sin have I committed
That still you send this punishment upon me?

ALMACHILDES
'Tis but a gentle punishment, so take it.

[ALMACHILDES *embraces* AMORETTA, *using this as a cover for tucking the ribbon 'in her bosom'*]

AMORETTA
Why, sir, what mean you? Will you ravish me?

ALMACHILDES
What in the gallery? And the sun peep in? 40

21 *noddies* fools, simpletons

22 The twisted colours of the ribbon will make Amoretta turn her colours, i.e. surrender to Almachildes.

23 *venery* See I.i.88.

24 *vintner* wine-merchant

29 *with a vengeance!* an expletive. Almachildes rejects these gifts as filthy: the ribbon is clean.

30 *nethermost* ed. (hethermost MS) The phrase 'the nethermost part of a wolf's tail' appears in Scot 6.7, a section which includes 'the brain of a cat' (see l. 28) and 'a little fish called *Remora*' (see I.ii.206–8).

31 *this* the ribbon charm

32 *cleanly* neat

38 s.d. 2 *bosom* the bodice, part of dress which covers the breast, and which was sometimes used as a place to put money or letters

40 *gallery* an indication of where the scene is supposed to be taking place

There's fitter time and place. [*Aside*] 'Tis in her bosom now.

AMORETTA

Go, you're the rudest thing e'er came at court.

ALMACHILDES

Well, well; I hope you'll tell me another tale
Ere you be two hours older. A rude thing?
I'll make you eat your word – I'll make all split else. 45

Exit

AMORETTA

Nay, now I think on't better, I'm to blame too.
There's not a sweeter gentleman in court –
Nobly descended too, and dances well.
Beshrew my heart, I'll take him when there's time;
He will be catched up quickly. The duchess says 50
She's some employment for him and has sworn me
To use my best art in't. Life of my joys,
There were good stuff! I will not trust her with him.
I'll call him back again. He must not keep
Out of my sight so long; I shall grow mad then. 55

Enter DUCHESS

DUCHESS

[*Aside*] He lives not now to see tomorrow spent,
If this means take effect, as there's no hardness in't.
Last night he played his horrid game again,
Came to my bedside at the full of midnight,
And in his hand that fatal, fearful cup, 60
Waked me and forced me pledge him, to my trembling,
And my dead father's scorn. That wounds my sight,
That his remembrance should be raised in spite.
But either his confusion or mine ends it.
[*To* AMORETTA] Oh Amoretta hast thou met him yet? 65
Speak, wench, hast done that for me?

AMORETTA

What, good madam?

41 *bosom* See l. 38 s.d. 42 *rudest* roughest, most barbarous
45 *split* break up, become wrecked
49 *take* capture
when while
50 *catched* in marriage 56 *He* the duke
62 *my . . . scorn* i.e. in scorn of my dead father
64 *his* the duke's
confusion overthrow, ruin
65 *him* Almachildes

DUCHESS
Destruction of my hopes! Dost ask that now?
Didst thou not swear to me, out of thy hate
To Almachildes, thou'dst dissemble him
A loving entertainment and a meeting 70
Where I should work my will?

AMORETTA Good madam, pardon me.
A loving entertainment I do protest
Myself to give him – with all speed I can too!
But as I'm yet a maid, a perfect one,
As the old time was wont to afford when 75
There was few tricks and little cunning stirring,
I can dissemble none that will serve your turn;
He must have e'en a right one and a plain one.

DUCHESS
Thou mak'st me doubt thy health. Speak, art thou well?

AMORETTA
Oh never better, if he would make haste 80
And come back quickly! He stays now too long.

[*The ribbon falls from* AMORETTA*'s clothes*]

DUCHESS
[*Aside*] I'm quite lost in this woman. What's that fell
Out of her bosom now? Some love-token?

[DUCHESS *picks up ribbon*]

AMORETTA
Nay, I'll say that for him: he's the uncivilest gentleman
And every way desertless.

DUCHESS [*Aside*] Who's that now 85
She discommends so fast?

AMORETTA I could not love him, madam,
Of any man in court.

DUCHESS What's he now, prithee?

AMORETTA
Who should it be but Almachildes, madam?
I never hated man so deeply yet.

DUCHESS
As Almachildes?

AMORETTA I am sick, good madam, 90

70 *entertainment* welcome, attention
78 *one* entertainment

When I but hear him named.

DUCHESS How is this possible?

But now thou saidst thou lovedst him and didst raise him
'Bove all the court in praises.

AMORETTA How great people
May speak their pleasure madam! But surely I
Should think the worse of my tongue while I lived then. 95

DUCHESS

No longer have I patience to forbear thee,
Thou that retain'st an envious soul to goodness!
He is a gentleman deserves as much
As ever fortune yet bestowed on man:
The glory and prime lustre of our court. 100
Nor can there any but ourself be worthy of him –
And take you notice of that now from me,
Say you have warning on't. If you did love him,
You must not now.

AMORETTA Let your grace never fear it.

DUCHESS

Thy name is Amoretta, as ours is; 105
'T has made me love and trust thee.

AMORETTA And my faithfulness
Has appeared well i'th' proof still, has't not madam?

DUCHESS

But if't fail now, 'tis nothing.

AMORETTA Then it shall not.
I know he will not be long from fluttering
About this place, now he's had a sight of me, and I'll perform 110
In all that I vowed, madam, faithfully.

DUCHESS

Then am I blessed both in revenge and love,
And thou shalt taste the sweetness. *Exit*

AMORETTA What your aims be
I list not to inquire. All I desire
Is to preserve a competent honesty 115

95 *then* if that were true

96 *forbear* endure, submit to

105 In the source the duchess is named Rosamunda. Middleton's change of name results in an extremely strained effect. See Introduction, p. xvi.

113 MS has Almachildes enter here.

114 *list* like

Both for mine own and his use that shall have me,
Whose luck soe'er it be.

Enter ALMACHILDES

Oh he's returned already.
I knew he would not fail.

ALMACHILDES [*Aside*] It works by this time
Or the devil's in't, I think. I'll ne'er trust witch else,
Nor sup with 'em this twelve month.

AMORETTA [*Aside*] I must soothe him
now, 120
And 'tis great pain to do't against one's stomach.

ALMACHILDES
Now Amoretta!

AMORETTA Now you're welcome, sir,
If you'd come always thus.

ALMACHILDES Oh am I so?
Is the case altered since?

AMORETTA If you'd be ruled,
And know your times, 'twere somewhat – a great
comfort. 125
'Las, I could be as loving and as venturous
As any woman – we're all flesh and blood man –
If you could play the game out modestly
And not betray your hand. I must have care sir;
You know I have a marriage-time to come, 130
And that's for life. Your best folks will be merry
But look to the main chance – that's reputation –
And then do what they list.

ALMACHILDES Wilt hear my oath?
By the sweet health of youth, I will be careful
And never prate on't, nor, like a cunning snarer, 135
Make thy clipped name the bird to call in others.

116 *have* in marriage
117 s.d. placed after l. 112 in MS
119 *the devil's in't* proverbial for something that is not working according to plan
124 *Is . . . since?* proverbial (see Tilley C 111)
ruled ed. (rude MS)
131 *best folks* See Introduction, p. xxiii.
135 *prate* chatter, boast of
136 *clipped* This has multiple meanings: a bird with clipped wings could not fly and was used to trap other birds; clipping coins, or paring the precious metal and selling it, mutilates the coin, just as an 'unchaste' woman would be seen to be mutilated; 'cleped' means named.

AMORETTA
Well, yielding then to such conditions
As my poor bashfulness shall require from you,
I shall yield shortly after.

ALMACHILDES I'll consent to 'em –
And may thy sweet humility be a pattern 140
For all proud women living.

AMORETTA They're beholding to you.
Exeunt

[Act II,] Scene iii

Enter ABERZANES *and an* OLD WOMAN [*carrying a baby*]

ABERZANES
So, so, away with him! I love to get 'em,
But not to keep 'em. Dost thou know the house?

[OLD] WOMAN
No matter for the house, I know the porch.

ABERZANES
There's sixpence more for that. Away; keep close.
[*Exit* OLD WOMAN]
My tailor told me he sent away a maidservant 5
Well ballast of all sides, within these nine days –
His wife ne'er dreamed on't – gave the drab ten pound
And she ne'er troubles him. A common fashion
He told me 'twas, to rid away a scape –
And I have sent him this for't. I remember 10
A friend of mine once served a prating tradesman
Just on this fashion, to a hair in troth.
'Tis a good ease to a man; you can swell a maid up
And rid her for ten pound; there's the purse back again,
Whate'er becomes of your money or your maid. 15

4 *close* secret
6 *Well ballast* weighted down, i.e. pregnant
6–12 Cf. the sanguine attitude towards child abandonment in CM II.ii.
7 *drab* harlot, strumpet
8–9 ed. (fashion: / He MS)
9 *rid away* get rid of
a scape trouble
11 *prating* See II.ii.135.
12 *to a hair* in precisely the same way
13 *swell* make pregnant
14 *rid her* get rid of the maid and of the baby
14–15 'Purse' may mean scrotum (see *The Taming of the Shrew* I.ii.54). The basic meaning, that men can get women pregnant with comparative impunity, is clear.

This comes of bragging now. It's well for the boy too.
He'll get an excellent trade by't and on Sundays
Go like a gentleman that has pawned his rapier.
He need not care what countryman his father was,
Nor what his mother was when he was gotten. 20
The boy will do well, certain – give him grace
To have a quick hand and convey things cleanly!
'Twill be his own another day.

Enter FRANCISCA

Oh well said!
Art almost furnished? There's such a toil always
To set a woman to horse, a mighty trouble. 25
The letter came to your brother's hands, I know,
On Thursday last by noon; you were expected there
Yesterday night.

FRANCISCA It makes the better sir.

ABERZANES
We must take heed we ride through all the puddles
'Twixt this and that now, that your safe-guard there 30
May be most probably dabbled.

FRANCISCA Alas, sir,
I never marked till now – I hate myself! –
How monstrous thin I look!

ABERZANES Not monstrous neither –
A little sharp i'th'nose, like a country woodcock.

FRANCISCA
Fie, fie, how pale I am! I shall betray myself. 35
I would you'd box me well and handsomely

16 *This comes of* this is what comes of
17 *on* ed. (one MS)
18 *Go like a gentleman* i.e. in a gentleman's clothes but without a rapier which gentlemen wore, therefore indistinguishable from a gentleman fallen on hard times and forced to raise cash by pawning his rapier
22 *convey* This suggests stealing from customers, something tailors were notorious for doing. *More Dissemblers Besides Women* V.i. suggests that tailors' sons were also proverbially dishonest.
23 *'Twill* the business will
well said! i.e. well done
24 *furnished* ready
30 *safe-guard* outer skirt worn to protect dress when riding
31 *probably dabbled* plausibly splashed, as if from a long journey
34 *woodcock* slang for fool
35 *betray myself* my looks will give the game away
36 *box me* slap my cheeks

To get me into colour.

ABERZANES　Not I, pardon me;
That let a husband do when he has married you;
A friend at court will never offer that.
Come, how much spice and sugar have you left now　40
At this poor one month's voyage?

FRANCISCA　Sure not much sir.
I think some quarter of a pound of sugar
And half an ounce of spice.

ABERZANES　Here's no sweet charge!
And there was thirty pound, good weight and true –
Beside what my man stole when't was a-weighing,　45
And that was three pound more, I'll speak with least.
The Rhenish wine, is't all run out in caudles too?

FRANCISCA
Do you ask that sir? 'Tis of a week's departure.
You see what 'tis now to get children sir.

[*Enter* BOY]

BOY
Your mares are ready both sir.

ABERZANES　Come, we'll up then.　50
Youth, give my sister a straight wand. There's twopence.

BOY
I'll give her a fine whip sir.

ABERZANES　No, no, no –
[*Aside*] Though we have both deserved it.

BOY　Here's a new
one.

ABERZANES
Prithee, talk to us of no whips, good boy;
My heart aches when I see 'em. Let's away.　55
Exeunt

39 *friend* See II.i.36.
41 *At* after
43 *no* ironic
46 *I'll . . . least* I would say at the lowest estimate
47 *caudles* warm, cordial drink
48 *'Tis . . . departure* it has been gone a week
51 *twopence* not a big tip. In *CM* I.i.80 even the ungenerous Yellowhammer tips a porter sixpence ($2\frac{1}{2}$p.).
54 *whips* Whipping was the usual punishment for whoring and so would be seen as an appropriate punishment for Francisca.

Act III, Scene i

Enter DUCHESS *leading* ALMACHILDES (*blindfold*)

ALMACHILDES
This's you that was a maid? How are you born
To deceive men! I'd thought to have married you;
I had been finely handled, had I not?
I'll say that man is wise ever hereafter
That tries his wife beforehand. 'Tis no marvel 5
You should profess such bashfulness to blind one,
As if you durst not look a man i'th' face,
Your modesty would blush so. Why do you not run
And tell the duchess now? Go, you should tell all.
Let her know this too. Why here's the plague now! 10
'Tis hard at first to win 'em; when they're gotten
There's no way to be rid on 'em; they stick
To a man like bird-lime. My oath's out.
Will you release me? I'll release myself else.

DUCHESS
Nay, sure, I'll bring you to your sight again. 15

[*Removes the blindfold*]

Say, thou must either die or kill the duke,
For one of them thou must do.

ALMACHILDES How, good madam?

DUCHESS
Thou hast thy choice, and to that purpose, sir,
I've given thee knowledge now of what thou hast
And what thou must do to be worthy on't. 20
You must not think to come by such a fortune
Without desert; that were unreasonable.
He that's not born to honour must not look
To have it come with ease to him; he must win't.
Take but into thine actions wit and courage, 25
That's all we ask of thee. But if through weakness
Of a poor spirit thou deniest me this,

1 *This's* ed. (This' MS)

3 *had* would have been
handled dealt with, i.e. deceived, as Almachildes would have been outraged if his bride (like the woman he has just had sex with) had lost her virginity

5 *tries* tests for virginity

11 *'em* women

13 *bird-lime* viscous, sticky substance, used for catching small birds
out up, expired

Think but how thou shalt die – as I'll work means for't,
No murderer ever like thee. For I purpose
To call this subtle, sinful snare of mine 30
An act of force from thee. Thou'rt proud and youthful;
I shall be believed. Besides, thy wantonness
Is at this hour in question 'mongst our women,
Which will make ill for thee.

ALMACHILDES I had hard chance
To light upon this pleasure that's so costly; 35
'Tis not content with what a man can do
And give him breath, but seeks to have that too.

DUCHESS
Well take thy choice.

ALMACHILDES I see no choice in't, madam,
For 'tis all death methinks.

DUCHESS Thou'st an ill sight then
Of a young man. 'Tis death if thou refuse it – 40
And say my zeal has warned thee – but consenting,
'Twill be new life, great honour and my love,
Which in perpetual bands I'll fasten to thee.

ALMACHILDES
How madam?

DUCHESS I'll do't religiously;
Make thee my husband. May I lose all sense 45
Of pleasure in life else, and be more miserable
Than ever creature was! For nothing lives
But has a joy in somewhat.

ALMACHILDES Then by all
The hopeful fortunes of a young man's rising,
I will perform it madam.

DUCHESS [*Kissing him*] There's a pledge then 50
Of a duchess' love for thee – and now trust me
For thy most happy safety. I will choose
That time shall never hurt thee. When a man

29 i.e. his death will be worse than that customarily meted out to a murderer

31 i.e. she'll claim he raped her
proud with a subsidiary sense, 'sexually potent'

36 *'Tis* chance or fortune is

37 *that* breath, i.e. instead of giving him a breathing space after sex, chance will, by taking away his breath, kill him

39 MS has 'Enter Gaspero', anticipating the beginning of the next scene.

40 *Of* for

43 *bands* marriage bands

49 *rising* with the innuendo 'have an erection'

53 *That time* a time for the murder

Shows resolution and there's worth in him,
I'll have a care of him. Part now for this time 55
But still be near about us till thou canst
Be nearer, that's ourself.

ALMACHILDES And that I'll venture hard for.

DUCHESS
Good speed to thee!

Exeunt

[Act III,] Scene ii

Enter GASPERO *and* FLORIDA

FLORIDA
Prithee be careful of me, very careful now.

GASPERO
I warrant you. He that cannot be careful of a quean can be careful of nobody; 'tis every man's humour that. I should ne'er look to a wife half so handsomely.

FLORIDA
Oh softly, sweet sir! Should your mistress meet me now 5
In her own house, I were undone for ever.

GASPERO
Never fear her. She's at her prick-song close;
There's all the joy she has or takes delight in.
Look, here's the garden key. My master gave't me
And willed me to be careful. Doubt not you on't. 10

FLORIDA
Your master is a noble, complete gentleman,
And does a woman all the right that may be.

Enter SEBASTIAN [*disguised as* CELIO]

SEBASTIAN
How now? What's she?

GASPERO A kind of doubtful creature –
I'll tell thee more anon.

[*Exeunt* GASPERO *and* FLORIDA]

SEBASTIAN I know that face

57 *ourself* The duchess is using the 'royal' we and playing on the notion that when they are married they will be as one person.

2 *quean* harlot, strumpet

7 *prick-song* written vocal music but also with a joke on Antonio's impotence and Isabella's current state of sexual frustration
close privately, secretly

To be a strumpet's – or mine eye is envious 15
And would fain wish it so where I would have it.
I fail if the condition of this fellow
Wears not about it a strong scent of baseness.
I saw her once before here, five days since 'tis,
And the same wary, panderous diligence 20
Was then bestowed on her. She came altered then,
And more inclining to the city-tuck.
Whom should this piece of transformation visit
After the common courtesy of frailty
In our house here? Surely not any servant; 25
They are not kept so lusty, she so low.
I'm at a strange stand. Love and luck assist me!
The truth I shall win from him by false play.

Enter GASPERO

He's now returned. [*To* GASPERO] Well, sir, as you were saying –
Go forward with your tale.

GASPERO What? I know nothing. 30

SEBASTIAN
The gentlewoman?

GASPERO She's gone out at back door now.

SEBASTIAN
Then farewell she, and you, if that be all.

GASPERO
Come, come, thou shalt have more. I have no power
To lock myself up from thee.

SEBASTIAN So methinks.

GASPERO
You shall not think, trust me, sir, you shall not. 35
Your ear; she's one o'th' falling family,
A quean my master keeps; she lies at Rutneys.

15 *envious* malicious
17 *condition* disposition, character
20 *panderous* pimping
22 *city-tuck* city fashion
23 *piece of transformation* Florida. Sebastian's comment, which suggests Florida's ability to transform herself so as to attract customers, reflects ironically on himself as he is currently 'transformed' by his disguise as Celio.
24 *After . . . frailty* according to the common conventions of whoring
26 *low* The image is both physical and social.
27 *strange stand* state of perplexity
36 *falling family* i.e. prostitutes

SEBASTIAN
Is't possible? I thought I had seen her somewhere.

GASPERO
I tell you truth sincerely. She's been thrice here
By stealth within these ten days, and departed still 40
With pleasure and with thanks sir; 'tis her luck.
Surely I think if ever there were man
Bewitched in this world, 'tis my master, sirrah.

SEBASTIAN
Thinkst thou so Gasper?

GASPERO Oh sir, too apparent.

SEBASTIAN
[*Aside*] This may prove happy. 'Tis the likeliest means 45
That fortune yet e'er showed me.

Enter ISABELLA [*with a letter*]

ISABELLA You're both here now,
And strangers newly lighted. Where's your attendance?

SEBASTIAN
[*Aside*] I know what makes you waspish. A pox on't!
She'll every day be angry now at nothing.

Exeunt [SEBASTIAN *and* GASPERO]

ISABELLA
I'll call her stranger ever in my heart. 50
She's killed the name of sister through base lust,
And fled to shifts. Oh how a brother's good thoughts
May be beguiled in woman! Here's a letter,
Found in her absence, reports strangely of her
And speaks her impudence. She's undone herself – 55
I could not hold from weeping when I read it –
Abused her brother's house and his good confidence.
'Twas done not like herself. I blame her much,
But if she can but keep it from his knowledge,
I will not grieve him first; it shall not come 60
By my means to his heart.

Enter GASPERO

Now sir, the news?

GASPERO
You called 'em strangers; 'tis my master's sister, madam.

43 *sirrah* a form of address indicating 'Celio's' inferior status
45 *likeliest* most promising
47 *newly lighted* just arrived, alighted (from horses)
52 *fled to shifts* resorted to expedients
58 *her* ed. (here MS)

ISABELLA
Oh is't so? She's welcome. Who's come with her?
GASPERO
I see none but Aberzanes. [*Exit*]
ISABELLA He's enough
To bring a woman to confusion, 65
More than a wiser man or a far greater.
A letter came last week to her brother's hands,
To make way for her coming up again,
After her shame was lightened – and she writ there
The gentleman her mother wished her to, 70
Taking a violent surfeit at a wedding,
Died ere she came to see him. What strange cunning
Sin helps a woman to!

Enter ABERZANES *and* FRANCISCA

Here she comes now.
Sister you're welcome home again.
FRANCISCA Thanks, sweet sister.
ISABELLA
You've had good speed.
FRANCISCA [*Aside*] What says she? [*To* ISABELLA] I have made 75
All the best speed I could.
ISABELLA I well believe you.
Sir we're all much beholding to your kindness.
ABERZANES
My service ever, madam, to a gentlewoman.
I took a bonny mare I keep and met her
Some ten mile out of town – eleven, I think – 80
'Twas at the stump I met you, I remember,
At bottom of the hill.
FRANCISCA 'Twas thereabout sir.
ABERZANES
Full eleven then, by the rod, if they were measured.
ISABELLA
You look ill methinks. Have you been sick of late?
'Troth, very bleak, doth she not? How think you sir? 85

65 *confusion* ruin
70 *wished her to* wanted her to marry
75 *had good speed* been successful, travelled quickly. Francisca's *Aside* expresses concern that her secret is out.
78 *service* a pun on sexual servicing
79 *her* Francisca
83 *rod* five and a half yards
85 *bleak* pallid, sickly

ABERZANES
No, no – a little sharp with riding; she's rid sore.
FRANCISCA
I ever look lean after a journey sister.
One shall do that has travelled, travelled hard.
ABERZANES
Till evening, I commend you to yourselves, ladies.
Exit
ISABELLA
[*Aside*] And that's best trusting to, if you were hanged. 90
[*To* FRANCISCA] You're well acquainted with his hand
went out now?
FRANCISCA
His hand?
ISABELLA I speak of nothing else; I think 'tis there.

[*Gives* FRANCISCA *the letter*]

Please you to look upon't, and when you've done,
If you did weep, it could not be amiss,
A sign you could say grace after a full meal. 95
You had not need look paler, yet you do.
'Twas ill done to abuse yourself and us,
To wrong so good a brother and the thoughts
That we both held of you. I did doubt you much
Before our marriage-day – but then my strangeness 100
And better hope still kept me off from speaking.
Yet may you find a kind and peaceful sister of me,
If you desist here and shake hands with folly,
Which you've more cause to do than I to wish you.
As truly as I bear a love to goodness, 105
Your brother knows not yet on't, nor shall ever
For my part – so you leave his company.
But if I find you impudent in sinning,
I will not keep't an hour, nay, prove your enemy
And you know who will aid me. As you've goodness, 110
You may make use of this; I'll leave it with you. *Exit*

86 *sharp* i.e. sharp-featured
88 i.e. one does look like that when one has hard travelling
travelled The MS spelling, 'travaild', makes clear the pun on 'travail': 1) labour; 2) give birth.
91 *hand* handwriting, also suggestion of physical intimacy
95 *full meal* i.e. the fulfilment of pregnancy (ironic in view of its sinfulness here)
100 *strangeness* newness, unfamiliarity
103 *shake hands with* say goodbye to
107 *his* Aberzanes'
110 *who* God as punisher of sin

FRANCISCA

Here's a sweet churching after a woman's labour
And a fine 'give you joy'! [*To the letter*] Why, where the devil
Lay you to be found out? The sudden hurry
Of hastening to prevent shame brought shame forth. 115
That's still the curse of all lascivious stuff;
Misdeeds could never yet be wary enough.
Now must I stand in fear of every look,
Nay, tremble at a whisper. She can keep it secret?
That's very likely, and a woman too! 120
I'm sure I could not do't – and I am made
As well as she can be for any purpose.
'Twould never stay with me two days – I've cast it –
The third would be a terrible sick day with me,
Not possible to bear it. Should I then 125
Trust to her strength in't, that lies every night
Whispering the day's news in a husband's ear?
No – and I have thought upon the means. Blessed fortune!
I must be quit with her in the same fashion
Or else 'tis nothing. There's no way like it – 130
To bring her honesty into question cunningly.
My brother will believe small likelihoods
Coming from me too. I, lying now i'th' house,
May work things to my will, beyond conceit too.
Disgrace her first, her tale will ne'er be heard. 135
I learned that counsel first of a sound guard.
I do suspect Gasper, my brother's squire there,
Had some hand in this mischief, for he's cunning
And I perhaps may fit him.

Enter ANTONIO

ANTONIO Your sister told me

112 *churching* religious service supposed to purify a woman after childbirth and resanctify her
113 *fine* ed. (five MS)
'give you joy' expression of greeting
117 proverbial. Cf. 'Murder will out', Tilley M 1315.
119–20 The notion that women cannot keep secrets was proverbial (Tilley W 649, W 701).
123 *cast* forecast, also vomited forth, i.e. told the news
134 *conceit* imagination
137 *squire* personal servant
139 *fit* get even with

You were come; thou'rt welcome.

FRANCISCA Where is she? 140

ANTONIO
Who, my wife?

FRANCISCA Ay, sir.

ANTONIO Within.

FRANCISCA
Not within hearing, think you?

ANTONIO Within hearing?
What's thy conceit in that? Why shak'st thy head so?
And look'st so pale and poorly?

FRANCISCA I'm a fool indeed
To take such grief for others, for your fortune, sir. 145

ANTONIO
My fortune? Worse things yet? Farewell life then!

FRANCISCA
I fear you're much deceived, sir, in this woman.

ANTONIO
Who? In my wife? Speak low; come hither softly sister.

FRANCISCA
I love her as a woman you made choice of –
But when she wrongs you, natural love is touched,
brother, 150
And that will speak, you know.

ANTONIO I trust it will.

FRANCISCA
I held a shrewd suspicion of her lightness
At first, when I went down, which made me haste the
sooner,
But more to make amends; at my return now
I found apparent signs.

ANTONIO Apparent, say'st thou? 155

FRANCISCA
Ay, and of base lust too – that makes th'affliction.

ANTONIO
There has been villainy wrought upon me then;
'Tis too plain now.

FRANCISCA Happy are they, I say still,
That have their sisters living i'th' house with 'em,
Their mothers or some kindred – a great comfort 160
To all poor married men. It is not possible
A young wife can abuse a husband then;
'Tis found straight. But swear secrecy to this, brother.

143 *conceit* idea
152 *lightness* wantonness

ANTONIO
To this and all thou wilt have.

FRANCISCA
Then this follows sir.

[FRANCISCA *whispers to* ANTONIO]

ANTONIO
I praise thy counsel well; I'll put't in use straight. 165

Enter ISABELLA

See where she comes herself.

[*Exit* FRANCISCA]

Kind, honest lady,
I must now borrow a whole fortnight's leave of thee.

ISABELLA
How sir, a fortnight's?

ANTONIO
It may be but ten days, I know not yet.
'Tis business for the state and 't must be done. 170

ISABELLA
I wish good speed to't then.

ANTONIO
Why that was well spoke.
I'll take but a foot-boy; I need no more.
The rest I'll leave at home to do you service.

ISABELLA
Use your own pleasure sir.

ANTONIO
Till my return
You'll be good company, my sister and you. 175

ISABELLA
We shall make shift sir.

ANTONIO
I'm glad now she's come –
And so the wishes of my love to both. *Exit*

ISABELLA
And our good prayers with you sir.

Enter SEBASTIAN [*disguised as* CELIO]

SEBASTIAN [*Aside*]
Now my fortune!
[*To* ISABELLA] By your kind favour madam.

ISABELLA
With me sir?

SEBASTIAN
The words shall not be many but the faithfulness 180
And true respect that is included in 'em

164 s.d. The substance of these whispered words can be deduced from IV.iii.3–4.
165 s.d. ed. (*l. 64 in* MS)
172 *foot-boy* attendant, page
176 *make shift* manage

Is worthy your attention, and may put upon me
The fair repute of a just, honest servant.

ISABELLA
What's here to do, sir? There's such great preparation
toward.

SEBASTIAN
In brief, that goodness in you is abused madam. 185
You have the married life but 'tis a strumpet
That has the joy on't and the fruitfulness;
There goes away your comfort.

ISABELLA How? A strumpet?

SEBASTIAN
Of five years' cost and upwards; a dear mischief,
As they are all of 'em. His fortnight's journey 190
Is to that country, if it be not rudeness
To speak the truth. I have found it all out madam.

ISABELLA
Thou'st found out thine own ruin; for to my knowledge
Thou dost belie him basely. I dare swear
He's a gentleman as free from that folly 195
As ever took religious life upon him.

SEBASTIAN
Be not too confident to your own abuse madam.
Since I have begun the truth, neither your frowns –
The only curses that I have on earth,
Because my means depends upon your service – 200
Nor all the execration of man's fury
Shall put me off. Though I be poor, I'm honest,
And too just in this business. I perceive now
Too much respect and faithfulness to ladies
May be a wrong to servants.

ISABELLA Art thou yet 205
So impudent to stand in't?

SEBASTIAN Are you yet so cold, madam,
In the belief on't? There my wonder's fixed,
Having such blessed health and youth about you,
Which makes the injury mighty.

ISABELLA Why I tell thee,
It were too great a fortune for thy lowness 210
To find out such a thing! Thou dost not look
As if thou'rt made for't. By the precious sweets of love,

190 *His . . . journey* Presumably Francisca has informed the servants of Antonio's impending absence.

191 *country* See I.i.92.

206 *stand* persist

I would give half my wealth for such a bargain,
And think 'twere bought too cheap. Thou canst not
guess
Thy means and happiness, should I find this true. 215
First, I'd prefer thee to the lord, my uncle;
He's governor of Ravenna; all the advancements
I'th' kingdom flows from him. What need I boast that
Which common fame can teach thee?

SEBASTIAN
Then thus
madam –
Since I presume now on your height of spirit 220
And your regard to your own youth and fruitfulness,
Which every woman naturally loves and covets –
Accept but of my labour in directions;
You shall both find your wrongs, which you may right
At your own pleasure, yet not missed tonight 225
Here in the house neither. None shall take notice
Of any absence in you, as I have thought on't.

ISABELLA
Do this, and take my praise and thanks for ever.

SEBASTIAN
As I deserve, I wish 'em and will serve you.

Exeunt

[Act III,] Scene iii

Enter HECATE, WITCHES [STADLIN, PUCKLE, HOPPO, HELLWAIN]; *and* FIRESTONE [*in the background, carrying eggs and herbs*]

HECATE
The moon's a gallant; see how brisk she rides.

STADLIN
Here's a rich evening, Hecate.

HECATE
Ay, is't not, wenches,
To take a journey of five thousand mile?

HOPPO
Ours will be more tonight.

HECATE
Oh 'twill be precious.
Heard you the owl yet?

STADLIN
Briefly in the copse 5
As we came through now.

HECATE
'Tis high time for us then.

216 *prefer* recommend
4–5 *Oh . . . yet* ed. (*one line in* MS)

STADLIN
There was a bat hung at my lips three times
As we came through the woods, and drank her fill;
Old Puckle saw her.

HECATE You are fortunate still;
The very screech-owl lights upon your shoulder, 10
And wooes you like a pigeon. Are you furnished?
Have you your ointments?

STADLIN All.

HECATE Prepare to flight then.
I'll overtake you swiftly.

STADLIN Hie thee Hecate;
We shall be up betimes.

HECATE I'll reach you quickly.
[*Exeunt all* WITCHES *except* HECATE]

FIRESTONE
[*Aside*] They're all going a-birding tonight. They talk of fowls i'th' air that fly by day; I am sure they'll be a company of foul sluts there tonight. If we have not mortality after it, I'll be hanged, for they are able to putrefy it, to infect a whole region. She spies me now. 15

HECATE
What, Firestone, our sweet son? 20

FIRESTONE
[*Aside*] A little sweeter than some of you or a dunghill were too good for me.

HECATE
How much hast here?

FIRESTONE Nineteen, and all brave plump ones,
Besides six lizard's and three serpentine eggs.

HECATE
Dear and sweet boy; what herbs hast thou? 25

FIRESTONE
I have some marmartin and mandragon.

8 *drank* The bat was a familiar and drank Stadlin's blood for nourishment.
12 *ointments* See I.ii.19–29.
13 *Hie* hasten
14 *betimes* in good time, speedily
15 *a-birding* behaving like birds, flying (though usually applying to bird-hunting)
17 *sluts* slatterns, dirty or slovenly women
18 *mortality* i.e. someone will be killed
23 *Nineteen* eggs
26 *marmartin* a comic malapropism for 'marmaritin', recalling the scandalous Martin Marprelate controversy (a religious pamphlet war that took place in the 1590s)

HECATE
Marmaritin and *mandragora* thou wouldst say.
Here's *panax* too; I thank thee.

FIRESTONE
My pan aches I am sure
With kneeling down to cut 'em.

HECATE
And *selago*,
Hedge-hyssop too. How near he goes my cuttings! 30
Were they all cropped by moonlight?

FIRESTONE
Every blade of 'em
Or I am a moon-calf mother.

HECATE
Hie thee home with 'em.
Look well to the house tonight; I am for aloft.

FIRESTONE
[*Aside*] Aloft, quoth you? I would you would break your neck once, that I might have all quickly! [*Music*] [*To* HECATE] Hark, hark, mother! They are above the steeple already, flying over your head with a noise of musicians. 35

HECATE
They are there indeed. Help, help me; I'm too late else.

Song

[VOICES OF WITCHES] *in the air*
Come away, come away;
Hecate, Hecate, come away. 40

HECATE
I come, I come, I come, I come,
With all the speed I may,
With all the speed I may.
Where's Stadlin?

[STADLIN] *in the air* Here.

27 *Marmaritin* See I.ii.161.
mandragora mandrake, narcotic plant with forked roots

28 The raised position of the s.h. FIRESTONE in MS means that the whole line is often attributed to him.
panax panacea, all-heal
pan socket, as of the thigh bone or knee cap, or short for 'brain pan' or skull

29 *selago* club moss

30 *Hedge-hyssop* medicinal plant

32 *moon-calf* congenital idiot

37 *noise* company or band of musicians

38 *there* ed. (they MS)

39–80 *Come away . . . reach* also used in *Macbeth* III.v.33 s.d. (see Introduction, pp. xii, xiv–xvi). See Appendix for music. Several of these lines are not attributed in MS, and any of the witches or Malkin have a claim to them. Malkin has to sing/mew some of them in a cat-like voice (easy enough with 'muse', 'refuse') for ll. 61–2 to make sense.

[HECATE]
Where's Puckle?
[PUCKLE] *in the air* Here – 45
And Hoppo too and Hellwain too;
We lack but you, we lack but you.
Come away, make up the count.
HECATE
I will but 'noint and then I mount.
[VOICES OF WITCHES] *above*
There's one comes down to fetch his dues: 50

[MALKIN] *a spirit like a cat descends*

A kiss, a coll, a sip of blood –
And why thou stay'st so long
I muse, I muse,
Since the air's so sweet and good.
HECATE
Oh art thou come? 55
What news, what news?
[MALKIN]
All goes still to our delight;
Either come or else
Refuse, refuse.
HECATE
Now I am furnished for the flight. 60
FIRESTONE
Hark, hark! The cat sings a brave treble in her own language.
HECATE *going up* [*with* MALKIN]
Now I go, now I fly,
Malkin my sweet spirit and I.
Oh what a dainty pleasure 'tis 65
To ride in the air
When the moon shines fair,
And sing and dance and toy and kiss.
Over woods, high rocks and mountains,

50 s.d. *descends* As with the later ascent with Hecate, this is a spectacular effect, but easily achievable in the Jacobean playhouse, where there was a winch in the roof which overhung the stage.

51 *coll* See I.ii.29.

61–2 *her own language* According to V.ii.31 this would be French. 'Oui' was thought to sound like a cat miaowing.

65 *dainty* precious

68 *toy* pet
Compare this line with I.ii.28–9.

Over seas, our mistress' fountains, 70
Over steeples, towers and turrets,
We fly by night, 'mongst troops of spirits.
No ring of bells to our ears sounds,
No howls of wolves, no yelps of hounds;
No, not the noise of water's breach 75
Or cannon's throat our height can reach.

[VOICES] *above*

No ring of bells to our ears sounds,
No howls of wolves, no yelps of hounds;
No, not the noise of water's breach
Or cannon's throat our height can reach. 80

FIRESTONE

Well mother, I thank your kindness; you must be gambolling i'th' air and leave me to walk here like a fool and a mortal. *Exit*

Act IV, Scene i

Enter ALMACHILDES

ALMACHILDES

Though the fates have endued me with a pretty kind of lightness, that I can laugh at the world in a corner on't, and can make myself merry on fasting nights to rub out a supper – which were a precious quality in a young, formal student – yet, let the world know, there is some 5 difference betwixt my jovial condition and the lunary state of madness. I am not quite out of my wits. I know a bawd from an aqua-vitae shop, a strumpet from wild-

70 *mistress' fountains* The moon (Diana, the goddess Hecate) affects the seas and controls fountains. Davenant has 'misty'.

71 *steeples* ed. (Steepe MS) See also the description of the witches flying at I.ii.22.

77–80 In MS the repeated lines are indicated by 'No Ring of Bells &c.'

1 *endued* endowed

3 *rub out* erase, do without

5 *formal* according to form, but also suggesting the forms students were divided into according to proficiency. The ability to be merry without supper would be an asset because of student poverty.

6 *lunary* lunatic, affected by the moon

7–9 *I know ... brimstone* Cf. *Hamlet* II.ii.378–9. Almachildes claims he can distinguish between things which are habitually closely associated.

8 *aqua-vitae* literally water of life, but also strong revivifying spirits such as whisky or brandy

8–9 *wild-fire* a name for erysipelas and other inflammatory diseases which spread easily

fire and a beadle from brimstone. Now shall I try the
honesty of a great woman soundly. She reckoning the 10
duke's made away, I'll be hanged if I be not the next
now. If I trust her, as she's a woman, let one of her long
hairs wind about my heart and be the end of me – which
were a piteous, lamentable tragedy and might be entitled
'A fair warning for all hair-bracelets'. 15
Already there's an insurrection
Among the people; they are up in arms –
Not out of any reason but their wills,
Which are in them their saints – sweating and swearing,
Out of their zeal to rudeness, that no stranger, 20
As they term her, shall govern over them.
They say they'll raise a duke among themselves first.

Enter DUCHESS

DUCHESS
Oh Almachildes, I perceive already
Our loves are born to crosses. We're beset
By multitudes – and, which is worse, I fear me 25
Unfriended too of any. My chief care
Is for thy sweet youth's safety.

ALMACHILDES [*Aside*] He that believes you not
Goes the right way to heaven, o'my conscience!

DUCHESS
There is no trusting of 'em; they are all as barren
In pity as in faith. He that puts confidence 30
In them dies openly to the sight of all men,
Not with his friends and neighbours in peace private,
But as his shame, so his cold farewell is,
Public and full of noise. But keep you close, sir,
Not seen of any, till I see the way 35
Plain for your safety. I expect the coming

9 *beadle* parish constable
brimstone sulphur, also hellfire
10 *She reckoning* a hint that the duke may not be dead
15 *'A fair ... hair-bracelets'* love tokens made from a lover's hair. Almachildes parodies moralistic play titles such as Heywood's *A Warning for Fair Women*.
20 *rudeness* roughness, ignorance
stranger foreigner
24 *crosses* thwartings, frustrations
28 *Goes ... heaven* is on a course to heaven, i.e. trusting the duchess will send him to hell
29 *'em* the people

Of the lord governor whom I will flatter
With fair entreaties to appease their wildness –
And before him take a great grief upon me
For the duke's death, his strange and sudden loss – 40
And when a quiet comes, expect thy joys.

ALMACHILDES
[*Aside*] I do expect now to be made away
'Twixt this and Tuesday night; if I live Wednesday,
Say I have been careful and shunned spoon-meat. *Exit*

DUCHESS
This fellow lives too long after the deed. 45
I'm weary of his sight; he must die quickly
Or I've small hope of safety. My great aim's
At the lord governor's love; he is a spirit
Can sway and countenance; these obey and crouch.
My guiltiness had need of such a master, 50
That with a beck can suppress multitudes,
And dim misdeeds with radiance of his glory,
Not to be seen with dazzled, popular eyes –

Enter L[ORD] GOVERNOR [*and* MESSENGER]

And here behold him come.

GOVERNOR [*To* MESSENGER] Return back to 'em;
Say we desire 'em to be friends of peace 55
Till they hear farther from us.

[*Exit* MESSENGER]

DUCHESS Oh my lord,
I fly unto the pity of your nobleness,
The grieved'st lady that was e'er beset
With storms of sorrows or wild rage of people.
Never was woman's grief for loss of lord 60
Dearer than mine to me.

GOVERNOR There's no right done
To him now, madam, by wrong done to yourself;
Your own good wisdom may instruct you so far –
And for the people's tumult, which oft grows
From liberty or rankness of long peace, 65

39 *take . . . me* feign a great grief
44 *spoon-meat* soft or liquid food taken with a spoon especially by infants or invalids, believed to have been used to poison Sir Thomas Overbury
49 *sway and countenance* be a commanding presence
51 *beck* gesture
52–3 Again the assumption is that 'great' people get away with murder.
53 *popular* of the common people
65 *rankness* excess in numbers and indiscipline or corruption. Regular war could be seen as healthy for a state; see *Coriolanus* IV.v.218–32.

I'll labour to restrain as I've begun, madam.

DUCHESS

My thanks and prayers shall ne'er forget you sir –
And, in time to come, my love.

GOVERNOR Your love, sweet madam?
You make my joys too happy! I did covet
To be the fortunate man that blessing visits, 70
Which I'll esteem the crown and full reward
Of service present and deserts to come.
It is a happiness I'll be bold to sue for
When I have set a calm upon these spirits
That now are up for ruin.

DUCHESS Sir my wishes 75
Are so well met in yours, so fairly answered
And nobly recompensed, it makes me suffer
In those extremes that few have ever felt –
To hold two passions in one heart at once,
Of gladness and of sorrow.

GOVERNOR Then as the olive 80
Is the meek ensign of fair, fruitful peace,
So is this kiss of yours. [*Kisses her*]

DUCHESS Love's power be with you sir.

GOVERNOR

[*Aside*] How she's betrayed her! May I breathe no longer
Than to do virtue service and bring forth
The fruits of noble thoughts, honest and loyal. 85
This will be worth th'observing and I'll do't. *Exit*

DUCHESS

What a sure happiness confirms joy to me,
Now in the times of my most imminent dangers!
I looked for ruin, and increase of honour
Meets me auspiciously. But my hopes are clogged now 90
With an unworthy weight; there's the misfortune.
What course shall I take now with this young man?
For he must be no hindrance. I have thought on't;
I'll take some witch's counsel for his end.
That will be sur'st. Mischief is mischief's friend. *Exit* 95

70 *that blessing* her love
75 *up* risen up in rebellion
79 Cf. *Hamlet* I.ii.10–13, *King Lear* IV.iii.17ff.
81 *ensign* sign, token
82 *of yours* of your peace
83 *her* herself

[Act IV,] Scene ii

Enter SEBASTIAN *and* FERNANDO

SEBASTIAN
If ever you knew force of love in life, sir,
Give to mine pity.
FERNANDO You do ill to doubt me.
SEBASTIAN
I could make bold with no friend seemlier
Than with yourself because you were in presence
At our vow-making.
FERNANDO I'm a witness to't. 5
SEBASTIAN
Then you best understand, of all men living,
This is no wrong I offer, no abuse
Either to faith or friendship – for we're registered
Husband and wife in heaven. Though there wants that
Which often keeps licentious man in awe 10
From starting from their wedlocks, the knot public,
'Tis in our souls knit fast – and how more precious
The soul is than the body, so much judge
The sacred and celestial tie within us
More than the outward form, which calls but witness 15
Here upon earth to what is done in heaven.
Though I must needs confess the least is honourable –
As an ambassador sent from a king
Has honour by the employment, yet there's greater
Dwells in the king that sent him – so in this. 20
FERNANDO
I approve all you speak and will appear to you
A faithful, pitying friend.

Enter FLORIDA

SEBASTIAN Look, there is she, sir,
One good for nothing but to make use of –
And I'm constrained to employ her to make all things
Plain, easy and probable. For when she comes 25
And finds one here that claims him, as I've taught

5 *vow-making* i.e. the betrothal between Isabella and Sebastian
12–20 Sebastian is arguing that a full marriage service would only be an earthly witness to the more important heavenly union which he and Isabella have already been through in their betrothal.
17 *least* i.e. the earthly marriage service
22 s.d. two lines earlier in MS
25 *she* Isabella 26 *him* Antonio

Both this to do't and she to compound with her,
'Twill stir belief the more of such a business.

FERNANDO
I praise the carriage well.

SEBASTIAN [*To* FLORIDA] Hark you, sweet mistress,
I shall do you a simple turn in this – 30
For she disgraced thus, you are up in favour
For ever with her husband.

FLORIDA That's my hope sir;
I would not take the pains else. Have you the keys
Of the garden-side that I may get betimes in
Closely and take her lodging?

SEBASTIAN Yes, I have thought upon
you. 35
Here be the keys. [*Gives keys*]

FLORIDA Marry and thanks, sweet sir.
Set me a-work so still.

SEBASTIAN [*Aside*] Your joys are false ones;
You're like to lie alone. You'll be deceived
Of the bedfellow you look for – else my purpose
Were in an ill case. He's on his fortnight's journey; 40
You'll find cold comfort there; a dream will be
Even the best market you can make tonight.
[*To* FLORIDA] She'll not be long now; you may lose no
time neither;
If she but take you at the door, 'tis enough.
When a suspect doth catch once, it burns mainly. 45

27 *this* Florida
she ed. (he MS) MS confuses his/her at IV.iii.36, so this emendation is plausible and it helps to make sense of an otherwise incomprehensible narrative: who would the 'he' be? If the 'she' is read as Isabella the meaning is that Isabella will 'compound' with Florida and so will already be half-convinced of the truth of Sebastian's allegations.
compound bargain, agree
29 *carriage* management
34 *garden-side* gate
betimes in good time
35 *Closely* See II.iii.4.
take take my place in
lodging Isabella's bedchamber. This results in Florida being stabbed by Antonio because of Francisca's plot.
42 *market* custom as prostitute
43 *you . . . neither* don't waste time
44 Cf. Francisca's plot, IV.iii.34.
45 *mainly* with force, vigour, violence. Cf. Tilley S 714: 'Of a little spark a great fire'.

There may you end your business and as cunningly
As if you were i'th'chamber, if you please
To use but the same art.

FLORIDA What need you urge that
Which comes so naturally I cannot miss on't?
What makes the devil so greedy of a soul 50
But 'cause he's lost his own, to all joys lost?
So 'tis our trade to set snares for other women
'Cause we were once caught ourselves. [*Exit*]

SEBASTIAN A sweet allusion!
Hell and a whore it seems are partners then
In one ambition. Yet thou'rt here deceived now; 55
Thou canst set none to hurt or wrong her honour –
It rather makes it perfect. [*He embraces* FERNANDO]
Best of friends,
That ever love's extremities were blessed with,
I feed mine arms with thee and call my peace
The offspring of thy friendship. I will think 60
This night my wedding-night, and with a joy
As reverend as religion can make man's,
I will embrace this blessing. Honest actions
Are laws unto themselves and that good fear
Which is on others forced, grows kindly there. 65

[*Knocking within*]

FERNANDO
Hark, hark! One knocks. Away sir; 'tis she certainly.
It sounds much like a woman's jealous 'larum.
[*Exit* SEBASTIAN]

Enter ISABELLA

ISABELLA
By your leave sir.

FERNANDO You're welcome gentlewoman.

ISABELLA
[*Aside*] Our ladyship then stands us in no stead now.
[*To him*] One word in private sir. [*Whispers to him*]

FERNANDO No, surely, forsooth, 70
There is no such here. You've mistook the house.

ISABELLA
Oh sir, that have I not; excuse me there,
I come not with such ignorance – think not so sir.

59 *feed* ed. (feele MS)

69 *ladyship* As an aristocrat Isabella is not used to being called by the lower-class title of 'gentlewoman'.

'Twas told me at the entering of your house here
By one that knows him too well.

FERNANDO
Who should that be? 75

ISABELLA
Nay, sir, betraying is not my profession –
But here I know he is, and I presume
He would give me admittance if he knew on't,
As one on's nearest friends.

FERNANDO
You're not his wife, forsooth?

ISABELLA
Yes, by my faith, am I.

FERNANDO
Cry you mercy then, lady. 80

ISABELLA
[*Aside*] She goes here by the name on's wife – good stuff!
But the bold strumpet never told me that.

FERNANDO
We are so oft deceived that let out lodgings,
We know not whom to trust. 'Tis such a world,
There are so many odd tricks nowadays 85
Put upon housekeepers.

ISABELLA
Why do you think I'd wrong
You or the reputation of your house?
Pray show me the way to him.

FERNANDO
He's asleep, lady,
The curtains drawn about him.

ISABELLA
Well, well, sir,
I'll have that care, I'll not disease him much. 90
Tread you but lightly. [*Aside*] Oh, of what gross falsehood
Is man's heart made of! Had my first love lived
And returned safe, he would have been a light
To all men's actions, his faith shined so bright.

Exeunt [ISABELLA *and* FERNANDO]

Enter SEBASTIAN [*disguised as* CELIO]

SEBASTIAN
I cannot so deceive her – 'twere too sinful. 95
There's more religion in my love than so.
It is not treacherous lust that gives content

79 *on's* of his
82 This confirms that Isabella has been talking with Florida.
90 *disease* disturb
92 *first love* This is the audience's first hint of the trick Antonio played on Isabella.

T'an honest mind – and this could prove no better.
Were it in me a part of manly justice,
That have sought strange, hard means to keep her
  chaste 100
To her first vow, and I t'abuse her first?
Better I never knew what comfort were
In woman's love than wickedly to know it.
What could the falsehood of one night avail him
That must enjoy for ever or he's lost? 105
'Tis the way rather to draw hate upon me;
For, known, tis as impossible she should love me
As youth, in health, to dote upon a grief,
Or one that's robbed and bound t'affect the thief.
No, he that would soul's sacred comfort win 110
Must burn in pure love like a seraphin.

Enter ISABELLA

ISABELLA
Celio?
SEBASTIAN Sweet madam?
ISABELLA Thou'st deluded me.
There's nobody.
SEBASTIAN How? I wonder he would miss, madam,
Having appointed too. 'Twere a strange goodness
If heaven should turn his heart now by the way. 115
ISABELLA
Oh never, Celio!
SEBASTIAN Yes, I've known the like.
Man is not at his own disposing madam;
The blessed powers have provided better for him
Or he were miserable. He may come yet.
'Tis early madam. If you would be pleased 120
To embrace my counsel, you should see this night over,
Since you've bestowed this pains.
ISABELLA I intend so.
SEBASTIAN
[*Aside*] That strumpet would be found, else she should
  go.
I curse the time now I did e'er make use
Of such a plague. Sin knows not what it does. 125
Exeunt

98 *this* i.e. the rape
109 *affect* feel affection for
117 Cf. Tilley M 298: 'Man proposes, God disposes'.

[Act IV,] Scene iii

Enter FRANCISCA *in her chamber* [*above*]

FRANCISCA
'Tis now my brother's time, even much about it;
For, though he dissembled a whole fortnight's absence,
He comes again tonight; 'twas so agreed
Before he went. I must bestir my wits now
To catch this sister of mine and bring her name 5
To some disgrace first, to preserve mine own.
There's profit in that cunning. She cast off
My company betimes tonight by tricks and sleights,
And I was well contented. I am resolved
There's no hate lost between us, for I know 10
She does not love me now but painfully,
Like one that's forced to smile upon a grief
To bring some purpose forward – and I'll pay her
In her own metal. They're now all at rest,
And Gasper there and all. List! [*Noise of snoring within*]
Fast asleep; 15
He cries it hither. I must disease you straight sir.
For the maidservants and the girls o'th' house,
I spiced them lately with a drowsy posset.
They will not hear in haste. [*Noise within*] My brother's
come!
Oh where's this key now for him? Here 'tis, happily – 20
But I must wake him first. Why Gasper, Gasper!

Enter GASPERO [*below*]

0 s.d. *chamber* bedchamber. Subsequent action makes clear this must be 'above'.
1 *time* the time he said he would arrive
5–6 Once Isabella is publicly dishonoured, no-one will believe her word, so Francisca will have nothing to fear from Isabella telling tales.
8 *betimes* early
sleights as in 'sleight of hand'
9 *resolved* convinced, certain
11 *but* except for
14 *In . . . metal* in kind
16 *cries* by means of his snores
disease discomfort
18 *spiced* i.e. drugged
posset See I.ii.85n. This recalls the preparations for the murder of Duncan in *Macbeth*.
21 *him* Gaspero

GASPERO
What a pox gasp you for?
FRANCISCA [*Aside*] Now I'll throw't down.
GASPERO
Who's that called me now? Somebody called 'Gasper'.
FRANCISCA
Oh up, as thou'rt an honest fellow Gasper.
GASPERO
I shall not rise tonight then. What's the matter? 25
Who's that? Young mistress?
FRANCISCA Ay; up, up, sweet Gasper.
My sister hath both knocked and called this hour,
And not a maid will stir.
GASPERO They'll stir enough sometimes.
FRANCISCA
Hark, hark again Gasper! Oh run, run, prithee!
GASPERO
Give me leave to clothe myself.
FRANCISCA Stand'st upon clothing 30
In an extremity? Hark, hark again!
She may be dead ere thou com'st. Oh in, quickly!
[*Exit* GASPERO]
He's gone. He cannot choose but be took now
Or met in his return; that will be enough.

Enter ANTONIO [*above*]

Brother? Here, take this light.
ANTONIO My careful sister. 35
FRANCISCA
Look first in his own lodging ere you enter.
[*Exit* ANTONIO]
ANTONIO
[*Within*] Oh abused confidence! Here's nothing of him
But what betrays him more.
FRANCISCA [*To* ANTONIO *within*] Then 'tis too true brother?
ANTONIO
[*Within*] I'll make base lust a terrible example;

22 *throw't* attempt, have a fling at the trick she is about to practise on Gaspero
25 *rise* i.e. sexually. See also 'stir' in 1. 28.
36 *his* MS corrects the original 'his' to 'her', but ll. 33–4 make it clear that it is Gaspero's absence from his bed that Francisca wants to be noticed. I therefore restore the original MS reading.
lodging bedchamber
37–8 *Here's . . . more* These lines are spoken in Gaspero's bedchamber, so his absence appears to confirm his guilt.

No villainy e'er paid dearer.

FLORIDA [*Within*] Help! Hold sir! 40

ANTONIO

[*Within*] I'm deaf to all humanity.

FRANCISCA List, list!

A strange and sudden silence after all.
I trust he's spoiled 'em both – too dear a happiness!
Oh how I tremble between doubts and joys!

[*Enter* ANTONIO *below, sword drawn*]

ANTONIO

There perish both – down to the house of falsehood 45
Where perjurous wedlock weeps! Oh perjurous woman!
She'd took the innocence of sleep upon her
At my approach and would not see me come,
As if she'd lain there like a harmless soul
And never dreamed of mischief. What's all this now? 50
I feel no ease; the burden's not yet off
So long as th' abuse sticks in my knowledge.
Oh 'tis a pain of hell to know one's shame.
Had it been hid and done, it'd been done happy –
For he that's ignorant lives long and merry. 55

FRANCISCA

[*Aside*] I shall know all now. [*To* ANTONIO] Brother!

ANTONIO Come
down quickly,
For I must kill thee too.

FRANCISCA Me?

ANTONIO Stay not long,
If thou desir'st to die with little pain.
Make haste I'd wish thee, and come willingly.
If I be forced to come, I shall be cruel 60
Above a man to thee.

FRANCISCA Why sir! My brother!

ANTONIO

Talk to thy soul, if thou wilt talk at all;
To me thou'rt lost for ever.

FRANCISCA This is fearful in you,
Beyond all reason brother. Would you thus

40 FLORIDA ed. (FRA. MS) I reject the MS wording as this would make nonsense of Francisca's plot. 43 *spoiled* destroyed, killed

44 s.d. Antonio can enter anywhere around the beginning of this speech; for theatrical effect it seems best to get him on quickly.

45 *house of falsehood* hell

54 Cf. *Macbeth* I.vii.1. 56–7 *Come . . . too* ed. (*one line in* MS)

Reward me for my care and truth shown to you? 65

ANTONIO

A curse upon 'em both and thee for company!
'Tis that too diligent, thankless care of thine
Makes me a murderer – and that ruinous truth
That lights me to the knowledge of my shame.
Hadst thou been secret, then had I been happy 70
And had a hope, like man, of joys to come.
Now here I stand, a stain to my creation,
And, which is heavier than all torments to me,
Have understanding of this base adultery –
And that thou toldst me first, which thou deserv'st 75
Death worthily for.

FRANCISCA If that be the worst, hold sir,
Hold brother! I can ease your knowledge straight,
By my soul's hopes, I can. There's no such thing.

ANTONIO

How?

FRANCISCA Bless me but with life, I'll tell you all.
Your bed was never wronged.

ANTONIO What! Never wronged? 80

FRANCISCA

I ask but mercy as I deal with truth now.
'Twas only my deceit, my plot and cunning
To bring disgrace upon her – by that means
To keep mine own hid, which none knew but she.
To speak troth, I had a child by Aberzanes sir. 85

ANTONIO

How! Aberzanes?

FRANCISCA And my mother's letter
Was counterfeited to get time and place
For my delivery.

ANTONIO Oh my wrath's redoubled!

FRANCISCA

At my return she could speak all my folly
And blamed me with good counsel. I, for fear 90
It should be made known, thus rewarded her,
Wrought you into suspicion without cause,

68 *ruinous* ed. (Ruynes MS)

71 i.e. before committing murder, Antonio, like humankind in general, had a hope of redemption

74 *Have understanding* ed. (the vnderstanding MS) 'The' in MS could be a misreading of 'Ha''. 85 *I had* ed. (*elided in* MS)

89 *she* Isabella *speak* speak of

90 *blamed* reproached, censured

And at your coming raised up Gasper suddenly,
Sent him but in before you by a falsehood,
Which to your kindled jealousy I knew 95
Would add enough. What's now confessed is true.

ANTONIO
The more I hear, the worse it fares with me.
I've killed 'em now for nothing; yet the shame
Follows my blood still. Once more, come down.

[*Sheathing his sword*]

Look you, my sword goes up. Call Hermio to me. 100
Let the new man alone; he'll wake too soon
To find his mistress dead and lose a service.

[*Exit* FRANCISCA]

Already the day breaks upon my guilt;
I must be brief and sudden. Hermio!

Enter HERMIO

HERMIO
Sir?

ANTONIO
Run, knock up Aberzanes speedily. 105
Say I desire his company this morning
To yonder horse-race, tell him; that will fetch him –
Oh hark you, by the way . . . [*Whispers*]

HERMIO
Yes sir.

ANTONIO
Use speed now
Or I will ne'er use thee more – and perhaps
I speak in a right hour. My grief o'erflows; 110
I must in private go and vent my woes.

Exeunt

Act V, Scene i

Enter ANTONIO *and* ABERZANES

ANTONIO
You are welcome sir.

ABERZANES
I think I'm worthy on't,

94 *but in before* just before
98–9 *yet . . . still* Shame is still attached to Antonio's family 'blood' but it is relocated from wife to sister. 101 *new man* Sebastian in his disguise as Celio
102 *lose a service* i.e. become unemployed
105 *knock up Aberzanes* knock at Aberzanes' door to get him out of bed
0 s.d. ANTONIO ed. (SEBASTIAN MS) 1 s.h. ANTONIO ed. (SEBASTIAN MS)

For look you, sir, I come untrussed in troth.

ANTONIO

The more's the pity – honester men go to't –
That slaves should 'scape it. What blade have you got
there?

ABERZANES

Nay, I know not that sir. I am not acquainted greatly with the blade; I am sure 'tis a good scabbard and that satisfies me. 5

ANTONIO

'Tis long enough indeed, if that be good.

ABERZANES

I love to wear a long weapon; 'tis a thing commendable.

ANTONIO

I pray draw it sir.

ABERZANES It is not to be drawn. 10

ANTONIO

Not to be drawn?

ABERZANES

I do not care to see't. To tell you troth, sir, 'tis only a holiday thing, to wear by a man's side.

ANTONIO

Draw it, or I'll rip thee down from neck to navel, though there's small glory in't. 15

ABERZANES

Are you in earnest sir?

ANTONIO I'll tell thee that anon.

ABERZANES

Why what's the matter sir?

ANTONIO

What a base misery is this in life now!
This slave had so much daring courage in him
To act a sin would shame whole generations, 20
But hath not so much honest strength about him
To draw a sword in way of satisfaction.
This shows thy great guilt, that thou dar'st not fight.

2 *untrussed* without the points or laces, which fastened the hose to the doublet, done up

3 s.h. ANTONIO ed. (SEBASTIAN MS)

3–4 Aberzanes' claim he is 'worthy' prompts Antonio's thought that honester men than Aberzanes suffer the death penalty when men like Aberzanes escape.

6–9 *blade . . . scabbard . . . long weapon* bawdy

8 s.h. as in MS

ABERZANES
Yes, I dare fight, sir, in an honest cause.

ANTONIO
Why come then slave – thou'st made my sister a whore. 25

ABERZANES
Prove that an honest cause and I'll be hanged.

ANTONIO
So many starting-holes? Can I light no way?
Go to, you shall have your wish – all honest play.
[*To* FRANCISCA *within*] Come forth, thou fruitful wickedness, thou seed
Of shame and murder!

[*Enter* FRANCISCA]

Take to thee in wedlock 30
Baseness and cowardice – a fit match for thee!
Come sir, along with me.

ABERZANES
'Las, what to do?
I am too young to take a wife in troth.

ANTONIO
But old enough to take a strumpet though.
You'd fain get all your children beforehand 35
And marry when you've done. That's a strange course sir.
This woman I bestow on thee; what dost thou say?

ABERZANES
I would I had such another to bestow on you sir.

ANTONIO
Uncharitable slave! Dog! Coward as thou art,
To wish a plague so great as thine to any. 40

ABERZANES
To my friend, sir, where I think I may be bold.

ANTONIO
Down, and do't solemnly.

[FRANCISCA *and* ABERZANES *kneel*]

Contract yourselves
With truth and zeal or ne'er rise up again.
I will not have her die i'th'state of strumpet

27 *starting-holes* means of evasion, loopholes
light alight, settle on

28 *play* Multiple meanings include: sword play, which has been averted; sexual play that has taken place between Francisca and Aberzanes; the 'play' or false deal Antonio is now proposing.

Though she took pride to live one. Hermio, the wine! 45

[*Enter* HERMIO *with wine*]

HERMIO
'Tis here sir. [*Aside*] 'Troth, I wonder at some things
But I'll keep honest.

ANTONIO
So here's to you both now
[ANTONIO *drinks*]
And to your joys, if't be your luck to find 'em.
I tell you, you must weep hard if you do.
Divide it 'twixt you both. [*They drink*] You shall not need 50
A strong bill of divorcement after that,
If you mislike your bargain. Go, get in now;
Kneel and pray heartily to get forgiveness
Of those two souls whose bodies thou hast murdered.
[*Exeunt* FRANCISCA *and* ABERZANES]
Spread, subtle poison! Now my shame in her 55
Will die when I die; there's some comfort yet.
I do but think how each man's punishment
Proves still a kind of justice to himself.
I was the man that told this innocent gentlewoman,
Whom I did falsely wed and falsely kill, 60
That he that was her husband first by contract
Was slain i'th' field – and he's known yet to live.
So did I cruelly beguile her heart,
For which I'm well rewarded; so is Gasper,
Who, to befriend my love, swore fearful oaths 65
He saw the last breath fly from him. I see now
'Tis a thing dreadful t'abuse holy vows
And falls most weighty.

HERMIO
Take comfort, sir,
You're guilty of no death; they're only hurt,
And that not mortally.

ANTONIO
Thou breath'st untruths. 70

Enter GASPERO [*wounded*]

HERMIO
Speak, Gasper, for me then.

GASPERO
Your unjust rage, sir,

48–9 i.e. the only way to joy (heaven) is through repentance, weeping
50 *it* the wine
51 *bill of divorcement* suggestive of the Essex divorce
55 *poison* The audience now realises what the whispering between Antonio and Hermio was about at IV.iii.108.
60 *falsely . . . falsely* under false pretences . . . mistakenly 62 *i'th' field* in battle

Has hurt me without cause.

ANTONIO 'Tis changed to grief for't.

How fares my wife?

GASPERO No doubt, sir, she fares well,

For she ne'er felt your fury. The poor sinner

That hath this seven year kept herself sound for you, 75

'Tis your luck to bring her into th'surgeon's hands now.

ANTONIO

Florida?

GASPERO She. I know no other sir;

You were ne'er at charge yet but with one light horse.

ANTONIO

Why, where's your lady? Where's my wife tonight then?

GASPERO

Nay, ask not me sir. Your struck doe within 80

Tells a strange tale of her.

ANTONIO This is unsufferable!

Never had man such means to make him mad.

Oh that the poison would but spare my life

Till I had found her out!

HERMIO Your wish is granted sir.

Upon the faithfulness of a pitying servant, 85

I gave you none at all; my heart was kinder.

Let not conceit abuse you; you're as healthful,

For any drug, as life yet ever found you.

ANTONIO

Why here's a happiness wipes off mighty sorrows.

The benefit of ever-pleasing service 90

Bless thy profession!

Enter L[ORD] GOVERNOR [*with* ATTENDANTS]

Oh my worthy lord,

I've an ill bargain, never man had worse!

The woman that, unworthy, wears your blood

To countenance sin in her – your niece – she's false.

GOVERNOR

False?

ANTONIO Impudent, adulterous.

GOVERNOR You're too loud, 95

72 *for't* ed. (fo't MS) 75 *sound* healthy, free from venereal diseases

78 *light horse* courtesan 87 *conceit* apprehension

88 *For . . . drug* as far as any poison is concerned

89 *off* ed. (of MS)

93–4 Again the notion is that noble blood may enable sinners to get off almost scot-free.

And grow too bold too with her virtuous meekness.

Enter FLORIDA [*wounded*]

Who dare accuse her?

FLORIDA Here's one dare and can.
She lies this night with Celio, her own servant –
The place Fernando's house.

GOVERNOR Thou dost amaze us.

ANTONIO
Why here's but lust translated from one baseness 100
Into another. Here I thought to have caught 'em
But lighted wrong by false intelligence
And made me hurt the innocent. But now
I'll make my revenge dreadfuller than a tempest;
An army should not stop me or a sea 105
Divide 'em from my revenge. *Exit*

GOVERNOR I'll not speak
To have her spared if she be base and guilty.
If otherwise, heaven will not see her wronged;
I need not take care for her. Let that woman
Be carefully looked to, both for health and sureness. 110
[*To* FLORIDA] It is not that mistaken wound thou wear'st
Shall be thy privilege.

FLORIDA You cannot torture me
Worse than the surgeon does – so long I care not.
[*Exit* FLORIDA *guarded*]

[GOVERNOR]
If she be adulterous, I will never trust
Virtues in women; they're but veils for lust. 115
Exit [*with remaining attendants*]

HERMIO
To what a lasting ruin mischief runs!
I had thought I had well and happily ended all
In keeping back the poison, and new rage now
Spreads a worse venom! My poor lady grieves me –

110 *sureness* security, so that she can be later produced as a witness

111 *mistaken* taken for Isabella

113 *surgeon* Surgeons were notorious for the pain they inflicted and the infrequency with which they cured anyone.

114 [GOVERNOR] ed. (*still Florida's speech in* MS)
she Isabella

114–15 This sentiment shows the same misogyny and false logic as Hamlet's famous move from the particular to the general with 'Frailty thy name is woman!'

'Tis strange to me that her sweet-seeming virtues 120
Should be so meanly overtook with Celio,
A servant; 'tis not possible.

Enter ISABELLA *and* SEBASTIAN [*as* CELIO]

ISABELLA Good morrow Hermio.
My sister stirring yet?
HERMIO How, stirring forsooth!
Here has been simple stirring! Are you not hurt madam?
Pray speak; we have a surgeon ready.
ISABELLA How! a surgeon? 125
HERMIO
Hath been at work these five hours.
ISABELLA How he talks!
HERMIO
Did you not meet my master?
ISABELLA How! your master?
Why, came he home tonight?
HERMIO Then know you nothing.
Madam,
Please you but walk in, you shall hear strange business.
ISABELLA
[*To* SEBASTIAN] I'm much beholding to your truth now,
am I not? 130
You've served me fair; my credit's stained for ever!
Exit [*with* HERMIO]
SEBASTIAN
This is the wicked'st fortune that e'er blew.
We're both undone for nothing. There's no way
Flatters recovery now, the thing's so gross.
Her disgrace grieves me more than a life's loss. *Exit* 135

[Act V,] Scene ii

Enter DUCHESS, HECATE, FIRESTONE [*A cauldron onstage*]

HECATE
What death is't you desire for Almachildes?

121 *overtook* caught in an offence
127 ed. (Did . . . *Master* / *Is.* how . . . night? / *Her.* then . . . Madam MS)
134 *Flatters recovery* flatteringly suggests any hope of recovery
gross evident
0 *Scene ii* ed. (Sce[a].3[a] MS)

DUCHESS
A sudden and a subtle.
HECATE Then I have fitted you.
Here lie the gifts of both sudden and subtle;
His picture made in wax and gently molten,
By a blue fire kindled with dead men's eyes, 5
Will waste him by degrees.
DUCHESS In what time prithee?
HECATE
Perhaps in a moon's progress.
DUCHESS What? A month?
Out upon pictures, if they be so tedious!
Give me things with some life.
HECATE Then seek no farther.
DUCHESS
This must be done with speed, dispatched this night, 10
If it may possible.
HECATE I have it for you;
Here's that will do't. Stay but perfection's time
And that's not five hours hence.
DUCHESS
Canst thou do this?
HECATE Can I?
DUCHESS I mean so closely.
HECATE
So closely do you mean too?
DUCHESS So artfully, so cunningly? 15
HECATE
Worse and worse! Doubts and incredulities!
They make me mad. Let scrupulous greatness know –
Cum volui, ripis ipsis mirantibus amnes
In fontes rediere suos, concussaque sisto,
Stantia concutio cantu freta, nubila pello 20
Nubilaque induco, ventos abigoque vocoque,
Viperias rumpo verbis et carmine fauces,

2 *have fitted* I have what is fit for you
3 *gifts . . . subtle* The ingredients have the power to bring about sudden and subtle death.
4 See note at I.ii.46–7.
11 *may possible* understand 'be'
12 *Here's* ed. (her's MS)
14 *closely* secretly
17 *scrupulous* troubled with doubts
18–25 Scot 12.7 translates: 'The rivers I can make retire, / Into the fountains whence they flow, / (Whereat the banks themselves admire) / I can make standing water go, / With charms I drive both sea and cloud, / I make it calm and blow aloud. /

Et silvas moveo iubeoque tremiscere montes
Et mugire solum manesque exire sepulchris!
Teque, luna, traho. Can you doubt me then daughter? 25
That can make mountains tremble, miles of woods walk,
Whole earth's foundation bellow and the spirits
Of the entombed to burst out from their marbles,
Nay, draw yond moon to my involved designs?

FIRESTONE
[*Aside*] I know as well as can be when my mother's mad 30
and our great cat angry, for one spits French then and
th' other spits Latin.

DUCHESS
I did not doubt you mother.

HECATE
No? What did you?
My power's so firm, it is not to be questioned.

DUCHESS
Forgive what's past – and now I know th' offensiveness 35
That vexes art, I'll shun th' occasion ever.

HECATE
Leave all to me and my five sisters, daughter;
It shall be conveyed in at howlet-time.
Take you no care; my spirits know their moments.
Raven or screech-owl never fly by th' door 40
But they call in – I thank 'em – and they lose not by't;
I give 'em barley, soaked in infants' blood.
They shall have *semina, cum sanguine*,
Their gorge crammed full, if they come once to our house.
We are no niggard. 45

[*Exit* DUCHESS]

FIRESTONE
They fare but too well when they come hither. They ate

The vipers' jaws, the rocky stone, / With words and charms I break in twain / The force of earth congealed in one, / I move and shake both woods and plain; / I make the souls of men arise, / I pull the moon out of the skies'. Scot also quotes l. 22 in 12.15. Dyce points out that Middleton copied his Ovid (*Metamorphoses* 7. 199–207) from Bodinus, *De Magorum Daemonomania* (1590) 2.2, p. 130, because, like Bodinus, he missed out a line (which would be after l. 22 here): 'Vivaque saxa sua convulsaque robora terra' ('the rocky stone ... The force of earth congealed in one').

28 *marbles* tombs

29 *involved* convoluted, entangled

31 *French* Cf. III.iii.61–2.

38 *howlet* owlet

43 *semina, cum sanguine* seed with blood

up as much t'other night as would have made me a good, conscionable pudding.

HECATE
Give me some lizard's brain. Quickly Firestone!
Where's Grannam Stadlin and all the rest o'th' sisters? 50

FIRESTONE
All at hand forsooth.

[*Enter* STADLIN, HOPPO, HELLWAIN, PUCKLE *and* A WITCH]

HECATE
Give me marmaritin, some bear-breech. When?

FIRESTONE
Here's bear-breech and lizard's brain forsooth.

HECATE
Into the vessel –
And fetch three ounces of the red-haired girl 55
I killed last midnight.

FIRESTONE Whereabouts, sweet mother?

HECATE
Hip; hip or flank. Where is the *acopus*?

FIRESTONE
You shall have *acopus* forsooth.

HECATE
Stir, stir about, whilst I begin the charm.

A charm song about a vessel

Black spirits and white, red spirits and grey, 60
Mingle, mingle, mingle, you that mingle may.
Titty, Tiffin, keep it stiff in.
Fire-drake, Puckey, make it lucky.
Liard, Robin, you must bob in.

48 *conscionable* reasonable
49 Scot 6.7 mentions lizard's brain as a love charm.
50 *Grannam* grandmother
51 s.d. Hecate's 'five sisters' of l. 37 suggests that an extra witch is needed for this scene.
52 *marmaritin* See I.ii.160–1.
bear-breech brank-ursine, herbaceous plant
When? i.e. hurry up, when will you do this?
55 *red-haired girl* Red hair was supposed to indicate potential for evil; in Renaissance imagery Judas Iscariot had red hair.
57 *acopus* a soothing salve but in Pliny (see Dyce) a plant or a stone
60–73 These lines are used also in *Macbeth* (IV.i.43).
60–4 Cf. charm at I.ii.1–5.
64 *Liard* ed. (Liand MS)

Round, around, around, about, about – 65
All ill come running in, all good keep out!

[STADLIN]
Here's the blood of a bat.

HECATE
Put in that, oh put in that.

[HOPPO]
Here's libbard's bane.

HECATE
Put in a grain. 70

[STADLIN]
The juice of toad, the oil of adder.

[HOPPO]
Those will make the younker madder.

HECATE
Put in – there's all – and rid the stench.

FIRESTONE
Nay, here's three ounces of the red-haired wench.

ALL [THE WITCHES]
Round, around, around, about, about – 75
All ill come running in, all good keep out!

HECATE
So, so, enough. Into the vessel with it.
There 't hath the true perfection. I am so light
At any mischief – there's no villainy
But is a tune methinks. 80

FIRESTONE
[*Aside*] A tune! 'Tis to the tune of damnation then, I warrant you, and that song hath a villainous burden.

HECATE
Come, my sweet sisters; let the air strike our tune,
Whilst we show reverence to yond peeping moon.
Here they dance the witches' dance and exeunt

67–72 s.h. *Stadlin* ... *Hoppo* ed. (Witch 1 ... Witch 2 MS) Any of the witches on stage can take these lines, but Stadlin and Hoppo seem an obvious choice because they are speaking parts elsewhere. The MS lay-out and the rhyming of the lines suggest that these lines are all meant to be sung.

69 *libbard's bane* 'leopard's poison', a poisonous plant. Davenant has 'lizard's brain', which is plausible.

70 *a grain* Davenant (againe MS)

72 *younker* fashionable young man

75 ed. (all Round: around: around &c:/ . MS)

82 *burden* accompaniment or refrain

84 s.d. See Introduction, p. xxv, for a description of the witches' dance in *Masque of Queens*.

[Act V,] Scene iii

Enter L[ORD] GOVERNOR, ISABELLA, FLORIDA, FRANCISCA, ABERZANES, GASPERO, [SEBASTIAN *as* CELIO, SERVANTS]

ISABELLA
My lord, I have given you nothing but the truth
Of a most plain and innocent intent.
My wrongs being so apparent in this woman –
A creature that robs wedlock of all comfort
Where'er she fastens – I could do no less 5
But seek means privately to shame his folly.
No farther reached my malice – and it glads me
That none but my base injurer is found
To be my false accuser.

GOVERNOR This is strange,
That he should give the wrongs yet seek revenge. 10
[*To* SEBASTIAN] But, sirrah, you – you are accused here doubly:
First, by your lady, for a false intelligence
That caused her absence, which much hurts her name,
Though her intents were blameless: next, by this woman,
For an adulterous design and plot, 15
Practised between you to entrap her honour,
Whilst she, for her hire, should enjoy her husband.
Your answer?

SEBASTIAN Part of this is truth, my lord,
To which I'm guilty in a rash intent,
But clear in act – and she most clear in both, 20
Not sanctity more spotless.

[*Enter* HERMIO]

HERMIO Oh my lord!

GOVERNOR
What news breaks there?

HERMIO Of strange destruction;
Here stands the lady that within this hour

0 *Scene iii* ed. (Sce^a^.4^a^ MS)

0 s.d. MS includes an entrance for Hermio and an erased entrance for Antonio. Francisca and Aberzanes make no contribution to the scene.

3 *this woman* Florida

12 *intelligence* communication of knowledge

16–17 *her* . . . *her* . . . *her* Isabella . . . Florida . . . Isabella

Was made a widow.

GOVERNOR How!

HERMIO Your niece my lord.

A fearful, unexpected accident 25
Brought death to meet his fury; for my lord,
Entering Fernando's house like a raised tempest,
Which nothing heeds but its own, violent rage,
Blinded with wrath and jealousy, which scorn guides,
From a false trap-door fell into a depth 30
Exceeds a temple's height, which takes into it
Part of the dungeon that falls threescore fathom
Under the castle.

GOVERNOR Oh you seed of lust,
Wrongs and revenges wrongful, with what terrors
You do present yourselves to wretched man 35
When his soul least expects you!

ISABELLA I forgive him
All his wrongs now and sign it with my pity.

FLORIDA
Oh my sweet servant! [*Faints*]

GOVERNOR Look to yond light mistress.

GASPERO
She's in a swoon my lord.

GOVERNOR Convey her hence.
It is a sight would grieve a modest eye, 40
To see a strumpet's soul sink into passion
For him that was the husband of another.

[SERVANTS *help* FLORIDA *off*]

[*To* SEBASTIAN] Yet all this clears not you.

SEBASTIAN Thanks to heaven
That I am now of age to clear myself then.

[*Removes his disguise*]

GOVERNOR
Sebastian!

SEBASTIAN The same, much wronged, sir.

ISABELLA Am I certain 45
Of what mine eye takes joy to look upon?

26 *his* Antonio's

30 *depth* See Introduction, p. xxiii, for the allegorical, infernal aspect of Antonio's death. 32 *fathom* length of six feet

38 *light* morally 41 *passion* passionate grief

44 *age* i.e. now Isabella is a widow, it is an appropriate time/age for Sebastian to reveal his identity and claim her

SEBASTIAN
Your service cannot alter me from knowledge;
I am your servant ever.
GOVERNOR Welcome to life sir.
Gasper thou swor'st his death.
GASPERO I did indeed my lord,
And have been since well paid for't. One forsworn
mouth 50
Hath got me two or three more here.
SEBASTIAN I was dead, sir,
Both to my joys and all men's understanding,
Till this my hour of life; for 'twas my fortune
To make the first of my return to Ravenna
A witness to that marriage – since which time 55
I have walked beneath myself and all my comforts,
Like one on earth whose joys are laid above –
And though it had been offence small in me
To enjoy mine own, I left her pure and free.
GOVERNOR
The greater and more sacred is thy blessing; 60
For where heaven's bounty holy groundwork finds,
'Tis like a sea, encompassing chaste minds.

Enter DUCHESS

HERMIO
The duchess comes my lord.
GOVERNOR Be you then all witnesses
Of an intent most horrid.
DUCHESS [*Aside*] One poor night
Ends Almachildes now. 65
Better his meaner fortunes wept than ours,

47 Sebastian is relieved that being a servant to Isabella has not rendered him unrecognisable to her or placed him socially beyond the pale. There is also play on the meaning of 'serving in love'.
51 *two . . . more* mouth-shaped wounds
54 *Ravenna* ed. (Vrbin MS)
56 *beneath myself* beneath his rank, as a servant
61–2 i.e. heaven is so generous that, even where only the foundations of possible decency exist in particular souls, grace will flood them like a sea until it renders them wholly chaste
62 *'Tis* heaven's bounty is. This is glaringly inappropriate, given the witchcraft Sebastian has used to secure his happy ending.
65 *Ends* ed. (ever MS)
65–6 ed. (*one line in* MS)

That took the true height of a princess' spirit
To match unto their greatness. Such lives as his
Were only made to break the force of fate
Ere it came at us, and receive the venom. 70
'Tis but a usual friendship for a mistress
To lose some forty years' life in hopeful time
And hazard an eternal soul for ever;
As young as he has done't and more desertful.

GOVERNOR
Madam.

DUCHESS My lord? 75

GOVERNOR
This is the hour that I've so long desired.
The tumult's full appeased; now may we both
Exchange embraces with a fortunate arm
And practise to make love knots, thus –

[*The*] DUKE *is discovered* [*as if dead*]

DUCHESS My lord!

GOVERNOR
Thus, lustful woman and bold murd'ress, thus! 80
Blessed powers, to make my loyalty and truth so happy!
Look thee, thou shame of greatness, stain of honour!
Behold thy work, and weep before thy death –
If thou be'st blessed with sorrow and a conscience,
Which is a gift from heaven and seldom knocks 85
At any murderer's breast with sounds of comfort –
See this, thy worthy and unequalled piece;
A fair encouragement for another husband!

DUCHESS
Bestow me upon death sir; I am guilty,
And of a cruelty above my cause. 90
His injury was too low for my revenge.
Perform a justice that may light all others
To noble actions. Life is hateful to me,
Beholding my dead lord. Make us an one

67–8 *That . . . greatness* i.e. it is preferable that a meanly born person should suffer than the duchess, who is not only born great but also has a great spirit
74 *done't* ed. (done MS)
77 *tumult* the crowd risen in rebellion
79 *love knots* knot or bow of ribbon as a love token; also describes the 'knot' of the duke's folded arms
87 *piece* masterpiece (ironic)
91 *His injury* to the duchess, i.e. the abuse of her father's skull
92 *Perform* ed. (performes MS)
94 *an one* a union, as one

In death, whom marriage made one of two living, 95
Till cursed fury parted us. My lord
I covet to be like him.

GOVERNOR No, my sword
Shall never stain the virgin brightness on't
With blood of an adult'ress.

DUCHESS There, my lord,
I dare my accuser and defy the world, 100
Death, shame and torment. Blood I am guilty of
But not adultery, not the breach of honour.

GOVERNOR
No? Come forth Almachildes!

Enter ALMACHILDES

DUCHESS Almachildes?
Hath time brought him about to save himself
By my destruction? I am justly doomed. 105

GOVERNOR
Do you know this woman?

ALMACHILDES
I have known her better, sir, than at this time.

GOVERNOR
But she defies you there.

ALMACHILDES That's the common trick of
them all.

DUCHESS
Nay, since I am touched so near, before my death then,
In right of honour's innocence, I am bold 110
To call heaven and my woman here to witness.

Enter AMORETTA

My lord, let her speak truth or may she perish!

AMORETTA
Then, sir, by all the hopes of a maid's comfort
Either in faithful service or blessed marriage,
The woman that his blinded folly knew 115
Was only a hired strumpet, a professor
Of lust and impudence, which here is ready

101–2 The duchess is willing to admit to murder but not to allow her chastity to be impeached. Cf. *The Changeling* V.iii.60–82.

104 Cf. Tilley T 333: 'Time reveals (discloses) all things'.

107 *known* sexually

115 *blinded* blindfolded

116–17 The duchess and Amoretta, like Sebastian, both use and decry prostitutes.

To approve what I have spoken.

ALMACHILDES A common strumpet?

This comes of scarves! I'll never more wear
An haberdasher's shop before mine eyes again. 120

GOVERNOR

My sword is proud thou art lightened of that sin.
Die then a murd'ress only!

[DUKE *rises*]

DUKE Live a duchess!

Better than ever loved, embraced and honoured.

DUCHESS

My lord!

DUKE

Nay, since in honour thou canst justly rise, 125
Vanish all wrongs, thy former practice dies.
I thank thee, Almachildes, for my life,
This lord for truth, and heaven for such a wife,
Who, though her intent sinned, yet she makes amends
With grief and honour, virtue's noblest ends. 130
What grieved you then shall never more offend you –
Your father's skull with honour we'll inter,
And give the peace due to the sepulchre –
And in all times, may this day ever prove
A day of triumph, joy and honest love. 135

Exeunt

Finis

119 *scarves* the blindfold Almachildes had to wear in III.i

123 The preposterous nature of this line and the duke's next speech qualifies the 'happiness' of the play's ending.

125 *honour* The duchess's sexually intact state is again held to be far more important than her attempts at murder.

126 *practice* plot, conspiracy
dies is forgotten

APPENDIX

The music reproduced below is edited and arranged by Ian Spink and should be easy to use for non-specialists.[1] Those wishing to consult the original need Drexel MS 4357, No. 32 (used by Spink) or Bodleian Library MS Mus.b.1.f.21. for 'In a maiden-time professed' (*The Witch* II.i.125ff.) and Drexel MS 4175. Liiii (used by Spink) or Fitzwilliam MU.MS.782 for 'Come away' (*The Witch* III.iii.39ff.). Spink's use of Drexel as his copy text has recently been criticised by Nicholas Brooke in Appendix B of his edition of *Macbeth* (p. 225). Both songs and music which was possibly used for the witches' dance called for at V.ii.82 are reproduced in *La Musique de scène de la troupe de Shakespeare The King's Men sous le règne de Jacques 1er*, ed. John Cutts (revised ed. 1971). 'Come away, Hecate!' appears on a CD disc published by Virgin Classics (Veritas) entitled *Shakespeare's Lutenist: Theatre Music by Robert Johnson* (VC 7593212).

1 See John Wilson, 'In a maiden time professed', *Musica Brittanica* 33, ed. Ian Spink (p. 45), and Robert Johnson (?), 'Come away, Hecate!', *The English Lute Songs* II, 17, ed. Ian Spink (1974), pp. 58–61. I am grateful to Ian Spink and Stainer and Bell for permission to reprint the music.

In a maiden time profess'd

JOHN WILSON

3. Whilst the world continued good,
People lov'd for flesh and blood;
Men about them bore the dart
That would catch a woman's heart.
Women likewise, great and small,
With a pretty thing they call
Cunny, cunny, won the men;
And this was all the Cupid then.

Come Away, Hecate!

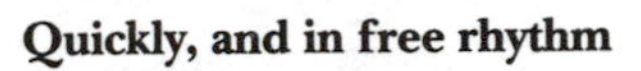

18
[Hecate]
Come a-way, make up the count. I will but 'noint, and then I mount,
22
[a Spirit like a cat decends: Spirit]
and then I mount, and then I mount. There's one come down to fetch his dues, A
26
kiss, a coll, a sip of blood; And why thou stay'st so long, I muse I muse,
31
[Hecate]
[Spirit]
Since the air's so sweet and good. Oh, art thou come? What news, what news? All goes

36
[Hecate]
well to our de - light: Ei - ther come or else re - fuse, re - fuse. Now I'm fur - nish'd
41
Faster
for the flight. Now I go, and now I fly, Mal - kin my sweet sprite and I;
46
Oh what a dain - ty plea - sure is this To ride in the air When the
50
moon shines fair; And feast and sing, and toy and kiss O - ver woods, high rocks and moun - tains,

55
O - ver seas, our mis - tress' foun - tains; O - ver steep - les, towers and tur - rets,
59
We fly by night, 'mongst troops of spi - rits. No ring of bells to our ears
64
sounds, No howls of wolves, nor yelps of hounds; No, not the noise of
71
wa - ter's breach, Nor can - non's throat our height can reach.